BRILLIANTLY
BIG
BUMPER

JOKE
BOOK

PUFFIN BOOKS

Published by the Penguin Group
Penguin Books Ltd, 80 Strand, London WC2R 0RL, England
Penguin Group (USA) Inc., 375 Hudson Street, New York, New York 10014, USA
Penguin Group (Canada), 90 Eglinton Avenue East, Suite 700, Toronto,
Ontario, Canada M4P 2Y3 (a division of Pearson Penguin Canada Inc.)
Penguin Ireland, 25 St Stephen's Green, Dublin 2, Ireland
(a division of Penguin Books Ltd)
Penguin Group (Australia), 250 Camberwell Road, Camberwell, Victoria 3124,
Australia (a division of Pearson Australia Group Pty Ltd)
Penguin Books India Pvt Ltd, 11 Community Centre, Panchsheel Park,
New Delhi – 110 017, India
Penguin Group (NZ), cnr Airborne and Rosedale Roads, Albany, Auckland 1310,
New Zealand (a division of Pearson New Zealand Ltd)
Penguin Books (South Africa) (Pty) Ltd, 24 Sturdee Avenue, Rosebank,
Johannesburg 2196, South Africa

Penguin Books Ltd, Registered Offices: 80 Strand, London WC2R 0RL, England

www.penguin.com

British Library Cataloguing in Publication Data
A CIP catalogue record for this book is available from the British Library

ISBN-13: 978–0–14132–040–3
ISBN-10: 0–141–32040–0

www.greenpenguin.co.uk

Mixed Sources
Product group from well-managed
forests and other controlled sources
www.fsc.org Cert no. SA-COC-1592
© 1996 Forest Stewardship Council

Penguin Books is committed to a sustainable future
for our business, our readers and our planet.
The book in your hands is made from paper
certified by the Forest Stewardship Council.

PUFFIN'S BRILLIANTLY BIG BUMPER JOKE BOOK

Illustrated by John Byrne

WELCOME, EVERYBODY!
AS THE FIRST LETTER IN
THE ALPHABET IT'S MY
DUTY TO KICK OFF THIS
GREAT JOKE COLLECTION...

HANG ON... IF THIS IS AN
`INTRODUCTION` THEN IT
SHOULD BE MY
JOB TO START
IT OFF...

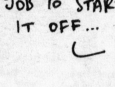

DID SOMEONE
SAY `START`...
THAT'S MY
WORD
SURELY?

PEOPLE SAY YOUR I.Q. SHOWS HOW CLEVER YOU ARE... BUT WE'RE TOO CLEVER TO FALL FOR THAT. WE LETTERS KNOW IT'S YOUR J.Q.* THAT COUNTS – AND WE'VE PUT LOTS OF GREAT GAGS IN THIS BOOK TO TEST YOU! HERE'S THE FIRST ONE ...
* J.Q. = HOW MANY JOKES YOU CAN QUOTE

AARDVARK

Knock, knock!

Who's there?
Aardvark.
Aardvark who?
Aardvark a million miles for one of your smiles!

ABANDON

First Sailor: Are you going to the dance?
Second Sailor: Dance? What dance?
First Sailor: There must be a dance – I just heard
someone yell "**A·band·on** ship".

ABBOT

Why don't monks smoke?

Because it could be **abbot** forming.

ACCIDENTS

A cowboy was being examined by his doctor.
'Yours is a very dangerous life,' said the doctor.
'Have you had many **accidents**?'
'Nope!' said the cowboy.
'Has nothing horrible ever happened to you?'
'Well, I was once kicked by my horse, and
another time a rattlesnake bit me.'
'Don't you call those accidents?' said the doctor
in amazement.
'Nope,' said the cowboy. *'They did it on purpose!'*

A man was in court for having caused a
road **accident**.
'When you arrived at the roundabout, what gear
were you in?' asked the judge.
'Well,' replied the man. *'I think it was green
trousers, a white shirt and these shoes.'*

ADAM

What did **Adam** say on the day before Christmas?
'It's Christmas, Eve!'

ADOPT

Why did the family **adopt** a flight of stairs?

Because they wanted some step children.

ADULTS

Why are **adults** always complaining?
Because they are groan ups!

AEROPLANE

Two men were sitting in an **aeroplane**.
'Look,' said one of them who was sitting by a
window. 'Those people down there are so tiny –
they look like ants.'
'*They are ants, you fool,*' said the other man,
'*we haven't taken off yet!*'

AGENT

What do you call an agent with two heads?
A double **agent**.

AILMENT

DOCTOR, DOCTOR, I think I'm a pint of beer.
Gosh that's a terrible **ale-ment**.

AIRLINE

What is the ghosts' favourite **airline**?
British Scareways.

ALARM

How do you stop someone stealing fast food?
Fit a burger **alarm**.

ALIEN

What's an **alien**'s favourite snack?
A Mars Bar.

ALLERGY

What happens if you have an **allergy** to bacon?
It brings you out in rashers.

ALLIGATOR

Knock Knock!
Who's there?
Althea.
Althea who?
Althea later, alligator!

ALPHABET

Man in restaurant: Waiter, there's a bee in my soup.
Waiter: Yes, sir, it's alphabet soup!

Father: Why are you taking so long with that
alphabet soup, son?
Son: I'm eating it alphabetically.

ANACONDA

What do you get if you cross an **anaconda** with a
glow worm?
A thirty-foot strip light!

ANDES

Teacher: Who can tell me where the **Andes** are?
Boy: I can – they're on the end of your armies!

ANIMALS

What **animals** like to play cricket?
Bats!

What big grey **animal** sits in rivers and complains that it's ill?
A **hippo-chondriac!**

ANTEATER

'I think my pet **anteater** is sad.'
'What makes you say that?'
'Well he's got such a long face...'

ANTI-FREEZE

Teacher: How do you make **anti-freeze**?
Boy: Lock her in the fridge!

APES

A small boy went into the kitchen and asked his mother: 'Mummy, my teacher says we are descended from the **apes**. Is that true?'
'I don't know, dear,' replied his mother, 'I never met your father's family!'

APPLE

DOCTOR, DOCTOR, I think I'm an **apple**.
Well sit down, I won't bite you!

Fascinating fact ➩ An **apple**
a day keeps the doctor away, an onion a day keeps
everyone away!

'An **apple** fell on top of my brother!'
'That can't have hurt much.'
'Yeah, but it was on its tree.'

APRIL

What day do ghosts hate the most?

April Ghouls day.

ARCHAEOLOGIST

DOCTOR, DOCTOR, I'm an **archaeologist**.
So what?
My career is in ruins!

ARCHER

What's a good first name for an **archer**?
Aim-y.

What's a good first name for an **archer** with no hair?

Archibald.

ARITHMETIC

What tool do you need for **arithmetic**?
Multi-pliers!

ASPIRIN

Why should you never leave a box of **aspirin** near a birdcage?
The parrots-eat-'em-all!

ASTRONAUT

How do you get a baby **astronaut** to go to sleep?
Rocket!

Where do **astronauts** keep their sandwiches?
In their launch box.

ATOM

One **atom** says to the other, 'I think I've lost an electron?'
'Are you sure?'
'Yes, I'm positive.'

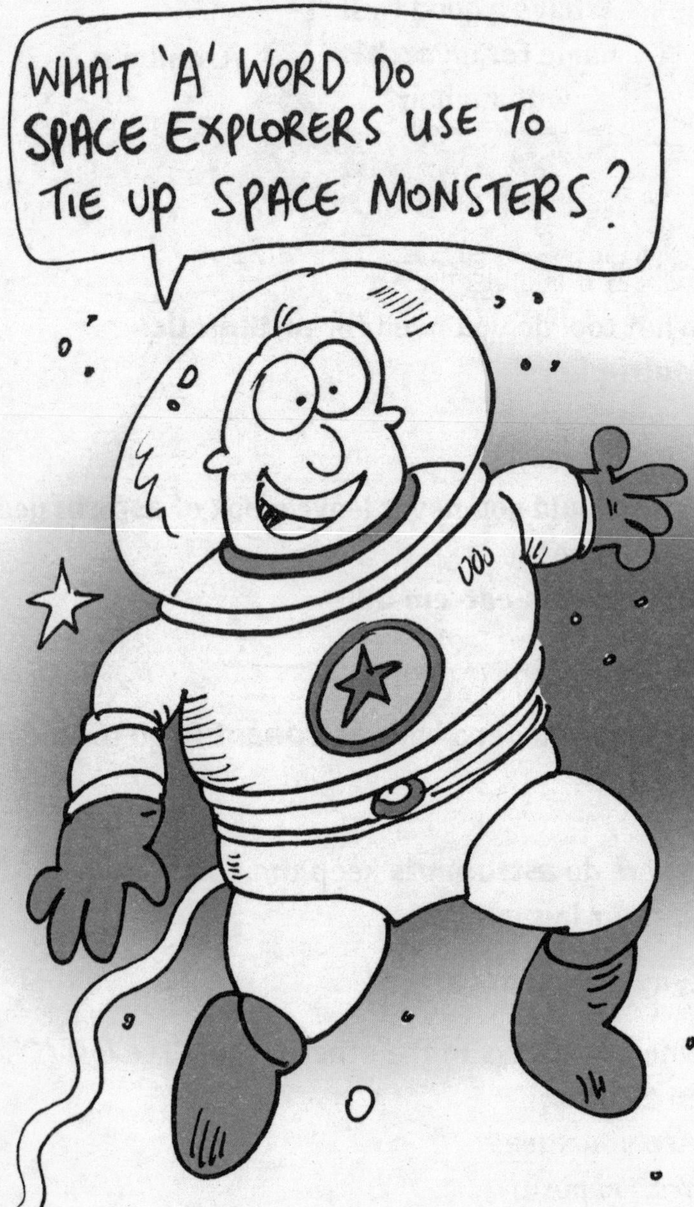
WHAT 'A' WORD DO SPACE EXPLORERS USE TO TIE UP SPACE MONSTERS?

AUTHORS

FALLING OFF A CLIFF by Eileen Dover

Get Rich Quick by Robin Banks

Expedition to the North Pole by Ann Tarctic

How to Feed Dogs by Nora Bone

THE TIGER'S REVENGE by Claude Leg

Be Prepared by Justin Case

KEEPING PET SNAKES by Sir Pent

GREAT MURDER MYSTERIES by Ivor Clue

MORE GREAT MURDER MYSTERIES by Hugh Dunnit

How to be a Waiter by Roland Butter

Ghost Stories by I. M. Scared

Chinese Window Cleaning by Who Flung Dung

SHIPWRECKS by Mandy Lifeboats

Daft Jokes by M. T. Head

BABY

What were the policeman's **baby's** first three words?
Hello! Hello! Hello!

When was Napoleon born?
When he was a baby.

BAGPIPES

Fascinating fact ➡ **Bagpipes** were invented by an ancient Scotsman who stood on an ancient Scottish cat's tail.

BALLERINAS

Why do **ballerinas** wear tu-tus?
Because three three`s are too big.

BALLOON

BANANA

If you can make shoes from crocodile skins, what can you make from **banana** skins?
Slippers!

BANANA SPLIT

What's a **banana split** called when you drop it from the top of a skyscraper on to the pavement below?
A banana splat!

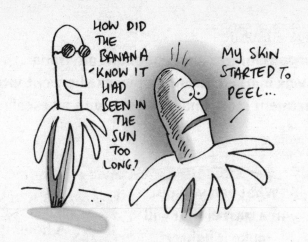

HOW DID THE BANANA KNOW IT HAD BEEN IN THE SUN TOO LONG?

MY SKIN STARTED TO PEEL...

BANDSTAND
How do you make a **bandstand**?
Hide all their chairs!

BANK
What do you call a man with a large overdraft at the **bank**?
Owen!

BARBER'S SHOP
A small cheeky boy went into a **barber's shop** and sat in a chair. 'Would you like a hair-cut, sonny?' said the barber.
'I'd like them all cut please!' said the boy.

BARBIE
What do you call five **Barbie** dolls standing in line?
A **Barbie** queue.

BARGAIN

A **bargain** hunter always bought anything that was marked down. Last week she went into a department store and came out with an escalator!

BARREL

What can you put in a **barrel** that will make it lighter?

A hole.

BARROW

What's long and slimy and good for carrying bags of cement in?
An eel-barrow.

BATH

Why did the robber take a **bath**?
So he could make a clean getaway!

BATHROOM

'Hey Dad, come quick, I've seen a horrible sight! Something is running across the **bathroom** floor – it's got no legs!'
'**What are you talking about, son?**'
'**Water!**'

BATSMEN

Why are **batsmen** cowards?
Because they are afraid of ducks!

BATTERING RAM

What's woolly and works in a chipshop?
A **battering ram**.

BEACH

What did the sea say to the **beach**?
Nothing, it just waved.

What washes up on tiny **beaches**?
Microwaves.

BEAMS

How do astronauts hold up the roofs of
their houses?
With moon **beams**.

BEAN

Man in restaurant: Waiter, what's this?
Waiter: It's **bean** soup, sir.
Man: I don't care what it's been, what is it now?

BEAR

Admiring lady: Have you ever hunted **bear**?
Hunter: No, I always wear a safari jacket and shorts.

THESE JOKES MIGHT BE TOO MUCH TO BEAR...

Fascinating fact ➡ If you cross a **bear** with a skunk, you get Winnie-the-Pooh.

The three **bears** came back from a teddy bears' picnic. 'Oh, no!' said Daddy Bear, 'Who's been eating my porridge?'
'And who's been eating MY porridge?' said Mummy Bear.
'*Never mind the porridge,*' said Baby Bear. '*Who's nicked the video?!*'

BEAUTY PARLOUR

A woman walked into a **beauty parlour** and said to the girl behind the desk: 'Have you got anything that might improve my looks?'
'*How about "distance"?*' said the girl.

BEEF

What do you call a thief who breaks into a meat factory?
A **beef** burglar.

BEES

Why do **bees** hum?
They don't know the words!

What do you call a **bee** with a quiet hum?
A mumble **bee**!

BEETROOT

What do you get if you cross vegetables with a drum kit?
Beat roots.

BELL

What do you get if you cross a **bell** with a bee?
A hum-dinger!

How do you dry a wet bell?

With a **bell** wringer.

BELLYBUTTON

DOCTOR, DOCTOR, I've got too much fluff in my **bellybutton**. Can you help me?
No, but you can help me - I've been wanting to restuff my couch for ages!

BENGAL

There was a young man from **Bengal**
Who went to a fancy dress ball,
He thought he would risk it,
And go as a biscuit,
But a dog ate him up in the hall!

BESTSELLER

'Have you read the werewolf's new book?'

'Yes, I hear it's become a **beast seller**...'

BICYCLE

Fascinating fact ➡️ A **bicycle** can't stand up on its own because it's too tired!

BILLIONAIRE

What was the **billionaire's** first name?
Rich.

BIRD

One little girl: My baby brother does **bird** impressions.
Another little girl: Really?
First little girl: Yes, he eats worms!

Why do **birds** fly south in the winter?
It's too far to walk!

What do you get if you cross a pet **bird** with a fierce dog?
A budgerigrrrrrr!

BIRTHDAY

A man reached his hundredth **birthday**. 'If I'd known that I was going to live this long,' he told his friends, 'I'd have taken better care of myself!'

What do you get every **birthday**?
A year older.

BLACK AND WHITE

What's **black and white** and red all over?
A newspaper!

What's **black and white** and red at the top?
A sunburnt puffin!

What's **black and white** and red at the bottom?
A badger with nappy rash!

What's **black and white** and black and white and black and white?
A nun rolling downhill!

BLOODHOUNDS

Newsflash: All the **bloodhounds** at Scotland Yard have been stolen. Police say they have no leads...

BLUEBOTTLE

'I must fly,' said the **bluebottle**.
'OK,' said the bee. '*I'll give you a buzz later.*'

BOA CONSTRICTOR

Why did the two **boa constrictors** get married?
They had a crush on each other!

BOATING LAKE

'Come in number 9!' called out a man working at
a **boating lake**.
'Hang on,' said his boss. 'We've only got seven
boats!'
'*Are you in trouble number 6?*' shouted the man,
looking worried.

BOOMERANG

How can you get rid of a **boomerang**?
Throw it down a one-way street!

What do you get if you cross a skunk with a
boomerang?
A smell that is very difficult to get rid of!

BOY

What is the difference between a **boy** and
a cowpat?
A cowpat stops being smelly after a couple of days.

BRAKES

A policeman overtook a motorist in an old car, and stopped him.

'Why were you going so fast?' he asked sternly.

'Well, officer,' said the driver, 'this car hasn't got any **brakes** so I was hurrying home before I had an accident.'

BRAZIL NUTS

Why are **Brazil nuts** so shy?

Because it's hard to get them out of their shell.

BRIDGE

Doctor, Doctor, I think I'm a **bridge**.

Now then, what's come over you?

So far, a bus and three cars.

BROTHERS!

A lady was putting her coat on to go out.

'Where are you going, Mum?' asked her daughter.

'I'm taking your **brother** to the doctor's; I don't like the look of him.'

'I'll come with you,' replied the girl. 'I don't like the look of him either!'

BUDGERIGAR

What should you do with a sick **budgerigar**?

Take it to a vet for tweetment!

BULLDOZER

What do you call a man with a **bulldozer** on his head?
Squashed!

BUM

What comes from the desert and shouts '**bum**!'?
Very crude oil...

BURGLAR

Judge: Why did you take all this money?
Burglar: I thought the change would do me good.

What do you get if you cross a **burglar** with a bag of cement?
A hardened criminal.

Why did the **burglar** get out of bed and give himself up?
He'd developed a quilty conscience.

BUTCHER

A lady went into a **butcher's** shop and bought some steak. Then she asked the butcher if she could have some bits for her dog.
'*Certainly, madam*,' said the Butcher. '*Which bits is he missing?*'

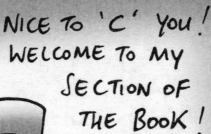
NICE TO 'C' YOU!
WELCOME TO MY
SECTION OF
THE BOOK!

HERE, YOU'LL FIND
LOTS OF GREAT JOKES
ABOUT THINGS BEGINNING
WITH 'C', LIKE FOR
INSTANCE... BOTTOMS?

'SCUSE ME!

CABBAGES

What do you call two rows of **cabbages**?
A dual cabbageway.

CACTUS

What did one **cactus** say to the other cactus?
'I do wish you didn't always have to be so prickly.'

CALCULATOR

Want to buy a pocket **calculator**?
No thanks – I already know how many pockets
I've got.

CAMEL

Why do **camels** wear sandals?
To stop themselves sinking into the sand.

Why do ostriches bury their heads in the sand?
To take a look at the **camels** who forgot to put
on their sandals!

What do you call a **camel** with three humps?
Humphrey!

Fascinating fact ➤ If you cross a
camel with a stupid cow you get thick, lumpy
milkshakes.

How do you disguise a **camel**?
With careful **camel**-flage.

CANDLES

I wish my brother wouldn't blow out the
candles on his birthday cake.
But he's supposed to blow out the candles on his
birthday cake.
Yes, but not with the vacuum cleaner.

CAPITAL

What **capital** city is like a stupid insect?
Antwerp.

CARETAKER

Why did the teacher marry the **caretaker**?
He swept her off her feet.

CARDS

Doctor, Doctor, I keep thinking I'm a pack
of **cards**.
Sit down, I'll deal with you later.

CARROTS

Why do rabbits eat **carrots**?
Well they can't drink them can they!

CARS

Why is a baby like an old **car**?
They both have a rattle!

Why can't **cars** play football?
They've only got one boot!

What do you call a man with a **car** on his head?
Jack!

CATS

What do **cats** like for breakfast?
Mice Crispies, of course!

What do you get if you cross a **cat** with a roast duck?
A duck-filled-fatty-puss!

Fascinating fact ➤ **Cats** are the only animals which change their size every day. You let them out at night and take them in every morning!

When is it unlucky to see a black **cat**?
When you're a mouse!

I bought a **car** once, but I took it back to the shop because, although the man there told me it would be good for mice, it never seemed to catch any. The shopkeeper said, 'Well, that's good for mice, isn't it?'

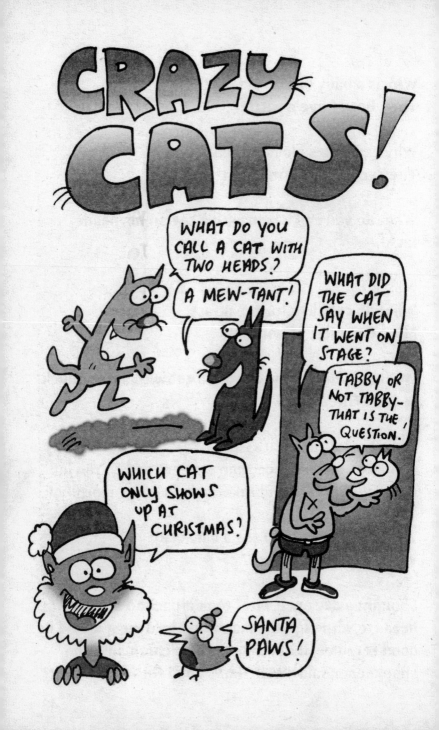

CHEATING

A teacher looked up from his desk while the children were doing an exam.

'James!' he said sternly. '**I hope I didn't just see you cheating**.'

'*So do I!*' said James.

CHICKEN

A man was driving his car along a lane past a cottage when a chicken ran out into the road. The man ran over it and killed it. Like a good chap he stopped the car and knocked on the cottage door.

'I'm terribly sorry, but I've just run over one of your chickens,' he said to the lady who opened the door. 'I'd like to replace it.'

'OK,' said the lady. '*How many eggs do you lay a week?*'

Lady (on phone to doctor): Doctor, I'm very worried, my husband keeps thinking he's turned into a **chicken**.

Doctor: Why didn't you tell me this before?

Lady: Well, *we've needed the eggs!*

Why did the **chicken** cross the road?
To get to the other side.

Why did the cockerel cross the road?
To show that he wasn't **chicken**.

Why did the dinosaur cross the road?
There weren't any **chickens** *in those days!*

Why did the elephant cross the road?
It was the **chicken's** *day off!*

CHICKS

Advert:
FOR SALE ONE-DAY-OLD **CHICKS** GOING CHEAP.

CHIP PAN

Newsflash: A mysterious object, shaped like a **chip pan**, was seen in the sky last night. The police say it may have been an Unidentified Frying Object.

CHIPS

A man sat down in a restaurant and ordered steak, **chips** and peas. The steak when it came was very small. When the man had finished a waiter came up and took his plate away. As he did so he asked: 'How did you find your steak, sir?' 'Easy,' said the man. '*I just moved a chip and there it was!*'

CINDERELLA

What song did **Cinderella** sing when she took her holiday films to the chemist's?
'Some day my prints will come...'

CINEMA

I took a seat in the local **cinema**...
The owners made me put it back.

CLOWN

Why did the monster spit the **clown** out?
He tasted **funny**.

COAL

What kind of bird digs for **coal**?

A mynah bird!

COAT OF ARMS

A **coat of arms** is what an octopus wears when it's cold.

COMEDIAN

Did you hear about the six foot eight **comedian**?
He liked to tell tall stories.

COMPOSER

Who is the most famous vampire **composer**?
Bite-hoven.

COOK

Knock Knock!

Who's there?
Cook.
Cook who?
You're the first one I've heard this year!

Small girl: Our school **cook** is very cruel, she beats the eggs and whips the cream.

COPPER NITRATE

Chemistry teacher: What's **copper nitrate**?
Boy: **What policemen on night duty get paid!**

COUNT

What's the fastest way to **count** cows?
Using a cowculator!

COURT

Order! Order in **Court**!
'I'll have fish and chips please, Guv,' said the prisoner.

COWBOYS

A **cowboy** was always claiming that he was the 'fastest gun in the West'. One day he came into a bar with his hands in plaster and his arm in a sling and a bandage round his head.

'What happened to you?' asked a man in the bar.

'I got beaten in a gun fight,' said the cowboy sadly.

'I thought you were the "fastest gun in the West"?'

'I am, *I was on holiday in the East when it happened!*'

COWS

Why do **cows** have bells?

Their horns don't work!

Fascinating fact ➡ **Cows** always lie down when it's raining. They do it to keep each udder dry.

Knock knock!

Who's there?

Cows.

Cows who?

No they don't, they moo!

What do you call a **cow** that eats your grass?

A lawn moo-er!

CRICKET

Why does the English **cricket** team need cigarette lighters?
They've lost all their **matches**!

CROCODILES

What is a **crocodile's** favourite game?

Snap!

A woman went into a shoe shop. 'I'd like a nice pair of **crocodile** shoes please,' she said.
'Certainly, *madam*,' said the assistant. '*What size shoes does the crocodile take?!*'

CURTAINS

Why should you always take a pencil up to bed with you?
So you can draw the **curtains**, of course!

DOCTOR, DOCTOR, I think I'm a pair of **curtains**.
Well, pull yourself together then!

NEVER MIND ALL THOSE D WORDS- I'M MORE INTERESTED IN WHY YOU D-CEIVED ME WHEN YOU SAID YOU'D TAKE YOUR TURN SWEEPING BACKSTAGE..
SO GET BACK HERE!
SORRY - I'M D-TOURING THROUGH THE NEXT FEW PAGES!

DAD

A girl came home from school and her **dad** asked if she'd had her homework marked. 'Yes, Dad,' she replied. 'I'm afraid you didn't do very well!'

DAFFODIL

What are the world's silliest flowers?

Daft·o·dils.

DANCE

What **dance** can you do in the bathroom?
A tap dance!

Where do snowmen go to **dance**?
A snowball.

DANCER

Knock! Knock!
Who's there?
Dancer.
Dancer who?
Dancer is simple, it's me.

DARTS

A man went into a pub with his dog and ordered a drink. Then he and the dog started playing **darts**!

'Hey, that's amazing!' said the barman. 'Your dog can play darts!'

'*It's not that amazing,*' replied the man. '*In the last ten games he's only beaten me twice!*'

DAYBREAK

Why should you keep a tube of glue under your pillow?

In case the **day breaks** while you're asleep.

DEAD HEAT

If a ghost and a vampire have a race who would win?

Neither - it would be a **dead heat**.

DEER

What do you call a **deer** with no eyes?

No eye deer!

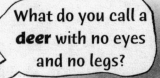

What do you call a **deer** with no eyes and no legs?

Still no eye deer!

DENTIST

What's the difference between a wet day and a boy at the dentist?
One pours with rain, the other roars with pain.

Carol's mum had just taken her to the **dentist** because she had a toothache. On the way home they dropped in on Carol's gran for a cup of tea.
'Is your tooth still hurting, dear?' asked the elderly lady, kindly.
'*I don't know,*' replied Carol. '*The dentist kept it!*'

DESERT

What do you call a snowman in a **desert**?

A wet patch in the sand!

DETECTIVE

Why did the detective spend the day in bed?
She was working undercover.

DIAMONDS

A mean man's girl friend said to him: 'Oh, darling, please buy me something with **diamonds** in it for my birthday.'
'*OK,*' said the man, '*How about a pack of cards?*'

DINNER

What's the difference between school **dinner** and pig swill?

School dinners come on a plate.

Knock knock!

Who's there?
Bernadette.
Bernadette who?
*Bernadette my **dinner**!*

DINNER LADY

Have you heard about the **dinner lady** who got an electric shock?
She stood on a bun and a currant shot up her leg!

DINOSAUR

Why did the **dinosaur** cross the road?
Because chickens hadn't evolved yet.

A boy was walking down the high street when he saw a huge **dinosaur** looking in a shop window. The boy put a long string round the dinosaur's neck and led him down the road to the police station. 'I've just found this stray dinosaur,' the boy said to a policeman on duty there. 'What should I do with him?'

'I think you should take him to the museum,' said the policeman. The next day the policeman was on point duty in the town when he saw the boy and the dinosaur walking down the street towards him.

'Hey, I thought I told you to take that dinosaur to the museum,' said the officer.

'I did,' said the boy. '*And today we are going to the cinema!*'

DISMAY

Knock knock!

Who's there?

Dismay.

Dismay who?

Dismay surprise you!

DOCTORS

DOCTOR, DOCTOR,
everyone ignores me.
Next!

DOCTOR, DOCTOR, I've only got fifty-nine
seconds to live!
Sit over there, I'll see you in a minute.

DOCTOR, DOCTOR, I'm at death's door.
Don't worry, I'll pull you through!

DOCTOR, DOCTOR, I've gone cricket crazy.
How's that?
Not out!

DOCTOR, DOCTOR, my wife thinks she's
a swallow.
Tell her to come and see me.
I can't, she's flown south for the winter!

DOCTOR, DOCTOR, I keep shrinking.
Well, you'll just have to be a little patient.

DOGS

What do trees and **dogs** have in common?
Bark!

A man went into his kitchen and saw his dog
sitting in the frying pan.
'What are you doing in there?' he asked.
'I'm a sausage dog,' replied the dog.

How do you stop a **dog** digging up your garden?
Take away his spade!

A man went into a pub with a poodle on a lead.
'This **dog** is a police dog,' he said to a friend.
**'Really?' replied the friend. 'It doesn't look much
like a police dog.'**
'I know,' said the man. *'It works in the plain clothes
division!'*

DOCTOR, DOCTOR, I think I'm a **dog**.
Sit down and tell me all about it.
I can't.
Why not?
I'm not allowed on the furniture!

Policeman: Has this **dog** got a licence?
Boy: No, he doesn't need one – he's too young
to drive.

ROLL UP! ROLL UP! FOR MY SPECIAL SECTION OF THE BOOK!
SEE A DOG WHICH TALKS JUST LIKE A PERSON!

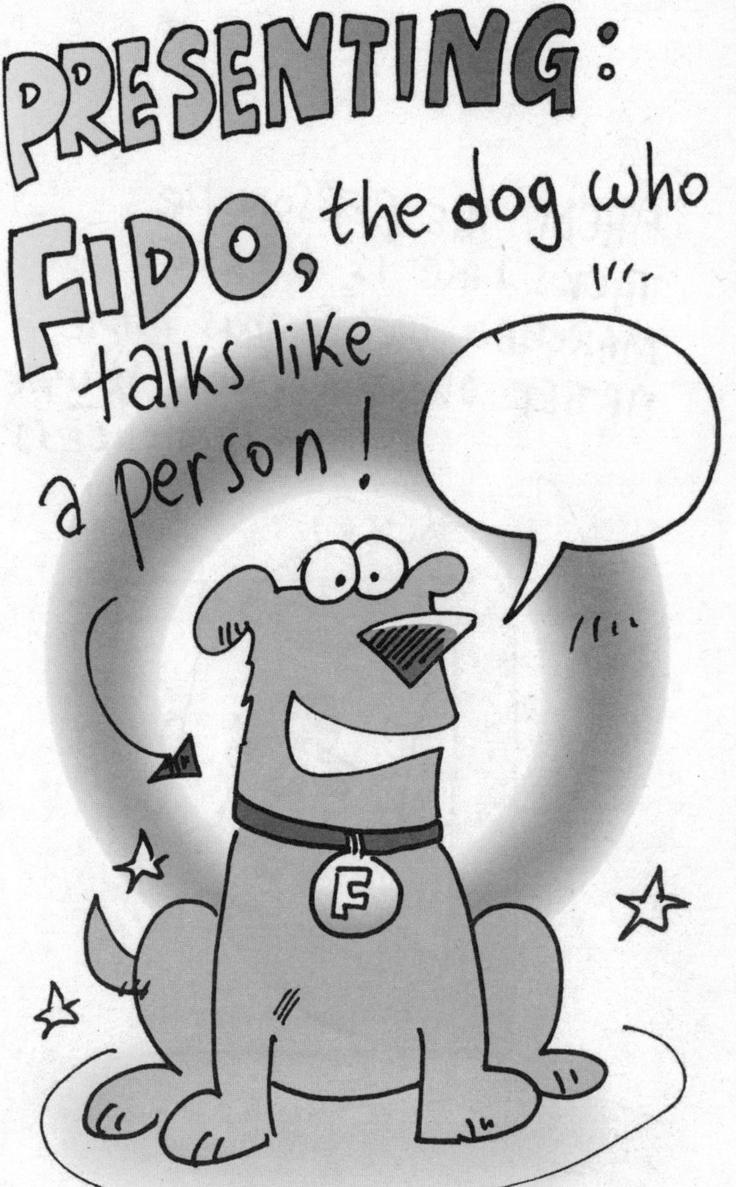
PRESENTING:
FIDO, the dog who
talks like
a person!
F

DOOR

When is a door not a door?
When it's ajar!

A boy went into the back garden and spoke to his mother: 'A man came to the **door**, Mum. He said he was collecting for the Children's Home.'
'Did you give him something?'
'Yes, my baby sister.'

DOUBLE VISION

A lady went to the doctor and complained that her eyesight didn't seem quite right. He inspected her and said: 'You've got **double vision**.'
'Don't be daft,' said the lady. *'I'm not taking any notice of you two!'*

DOWN

How do you get **down** from an elephant?
You don't, you get down from a duck!

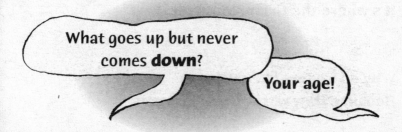

What goes up but never comes **down**?

Your age!

DRESS

Lady: Can I try on that **dress** in the window?
Shop assistant: I'd use a changing-room if I were you, madam!'

DRUM

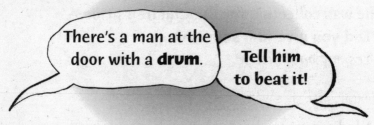

There's a man at the door with a **drum**.

Tell him to beat it!

DUCKS

Fascinating fact There's nothing a **duck** likes better than to put its webbed feet up, open a box of Cream Quackers and watch a ducku-mentary on TV. They like the feather forecast and great jokes quack them up!

DUST

Why is 10 Downing Street so **dusty**?
It's where the Grime Minister lives.

DUSTMEN

Why do waiters like **dustmen**?
Because they're such good tippers.

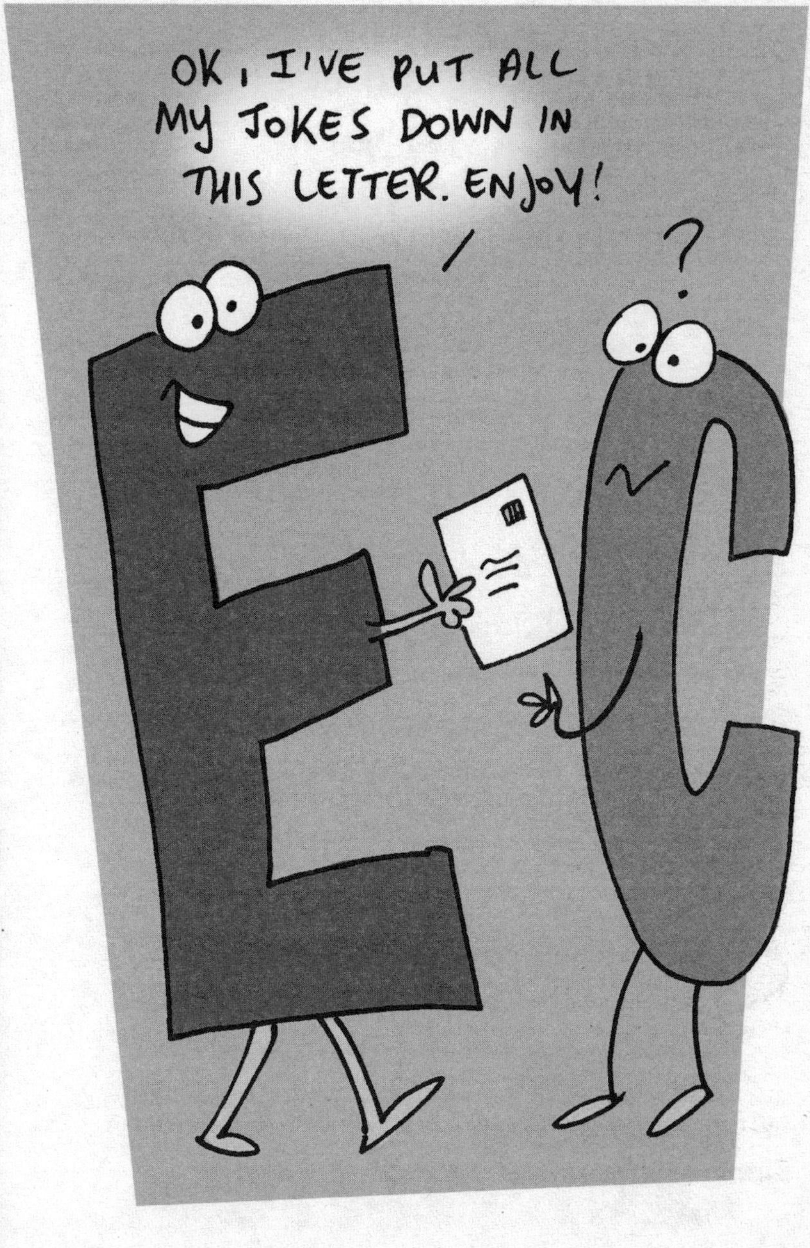
OK, I'VE PUT ALL MY JOKES DOWN IN THIS LETTER. ENJOY!
?

EARS

What kind of **ears** does an engine have?
Engineers!

EARTHQUAKE

What do you get if you cross a cow with
an **earthquake**?
A milkshake.

EARWIGS

Fascinating fact ➤ When **earwigs**
go to a football match they all chant '*Earwigo-ear-
wigo-earwigo!*'

EASEL

What did the painter say when she lost her
equipment?
'**Easel** come, Easel go!'

ECHO

What do you get when you shout into the door of
a henhouse?
An **egg-cho**.

ECLAIR

What do you call a French girl with chocolate
sauce on her head?
E-Clare.

EGGS

How do ghosts like their **eggs** cooked?
Petrifried!

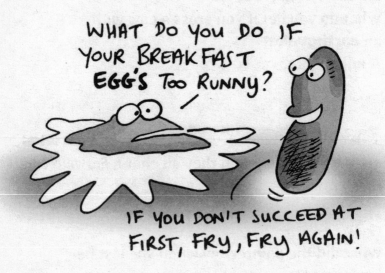

EIFFEL TOWER

Girl: I can jump as high as the **Eiffel Tower**.
Her friend: I bet you can't.
Girl: I can you know – the Eiffel Tower can't jump!

ELECTRICIAN

An **electrician** went to the pub and when he came home his friend said: 'Wire you insulate?'

ELEPHANT

How do you know if there's an **elephant** in your fridge?
Footprints in the butter!

Why is an **elephant** so wrinkled?

Have you ever tried to iron an elephant?

First **elephant**: Why do we have such good memories?
Second elephant: I forget.

What is as big as an **elephant** but doesn't weigh anything?
An elephant's shadow.

Two **elephants** went on holiday and sat down on the beach. It was a very hot day and they fancied having a swim in the sea. Unfortunately they couldn't: *they only had one pair of trunks!*

What would you get if you crossed an **elephant** with a kangaroo?
Holes in Australia.

TEST your J.Q. ...
Why didn't the ELK TAKE His MUM ON HOLiDAY?
MUM
Because if he had done the tickets would have been 'FOR TWO DEER'!

EMU

Why do **emus** read joke books?
For their own emu-sement.

ENVELOPE

What did the stamp say to the **envelope**?
'Stick with me and we'll go places!'

ESKIMOS

How does an **eskimo** keep the roof on his house?
'E glues it!

Fascinating fact ➤ An Ig is an **eskimo** house that hasn't got a toilet!

EXAM

'Please, sir, I've finished the **exam**,' said a girl.
'Good,' said the teacher. 'Did the questions give you any difficulties?'
'No,' she replied, 'but some of the answers did!'

A boy came home from school with his **exam** results.
'How did you get on, son?' asked his father.
'My marks were under water,' said the boy.
'What do you mean "under water"?'
'They were all below "C" level!'

'I've got some good news for you about my **exam** results,' said a girl coming home from school.
'**What do you mean?**' said her parents.
'Well, you know you said you'd give me ten pounds for every exam I passed – I've just saved you a lot of money!'

EXECUTIONERS

Fascinating fact In the olden days **executioners** knew who to execute because they had a chopping list.

EXERCISE

What is a cat's favourite **exercise**?
Puss ups.

EYE

What did one **eye** say to the other eye?

Between you and me something smells.

EYE TEST

A small girl was having an **eye test**. 'Can you read out the letters on the chart on the wall?' asked the optician.
'*What chart?*' replied the girl.

FAN

Why did the football team feel chilly?
Because they had so many fans.

FAST FOOD

Why do burgers wear skates?
Because they are fast food.

FATHER'S DAY

(FATHER'S DAY FOR JOKES THAT IS!)

HEY! WHO PUT GLUE ALL OVER THOSE LETTERS?

IT WAS ME, DAD...YOU SAID I SHOULD STICK AT MY SPELLING PRACTICE...

FEET

What wears shoes but has no **feet**?
A pavement.

What's the last thing you take off at night before going to bed?
Your feet - you take them off the floor and put them in the bed!

FELIX

Knock Knock!

Who's there?
Felix.
Felix who?
Felix my lolly once more I'm going to scream!

FIRE

Did you hear about the plastic surgeon who got too close to the **fire**?
He melted.

FIREPLACE

What king invented the **fireplace**?
Alfred the grate!

FIR TREE

What do you call a girl with a **fir tree** on her head?
Christmas Carol!

FISH

What do you call **fish** with no eyes?

F-S S S S H H H H!

What **fish** swims at a hundred miles an hour?
A motorpike!

What **fish** sleep a lot?
Kippers!

FISH AND CHIPS

A man went into a **fish and chip** shop and said:
'Fish and chips twice!'
'It's all right,' said the man behind the counter.
'I heard you the first time!'

FLAMINGOS

Teacher: Why do **flamingos** stand with one leg out
of the water?
Girl: If they took both legs out they'd fall in it!

FLEA

First **flea**: How are you?
Second flea: Not very well – I'm not feeling
up to scratch!

What did one **flea** say to other when they were on the dog's back?
'I'll hang around here fur a while, you go on a head!'

FLIES

Two **flies** were playing football in a saucer.
They were practising for the cup!

DOCTOR, DOCTOR, I keep thinking I'm a **fly**.
Well buzz off then.

Waiter, what's this **fly** doing in my soup?
I think it's doing breaststroke, sir!

FLOODLIGHTS

How did Noah find things inside the Ark?
He had floodlights.

FLOWER

What did the bee say to the **flower**?
Hello, honey!

FOG

What happens when there hasn't been **fog** for a while?
It's mist.

FOOTBALL

A boy was very late for school. 'Why are you so late?' said the Head Teacher sternly.
'I'm sorry,' said the boy. 'I was dreaming about **football**.'
'And why does dreaming about football make you late for school?'
'*They played extra time!*' said the boy.

First lady: My son has got into the school **football** team.
Second lady: What position does he play in?
First lady: *He's left back in the dressing room!*

When it stops rolling, does a **football** look round?

FOOTBALL SHORTS

A boy came home from school and told his father:
'My teacher says I need a new pair of **football shorts** for gym.'
'*Tell him he will have to get his own football shorts!*'

FORK

Did you hear about the man who got a puncture because there was a **fork** in the road?

FORTUNE

How can you get a small **fortune**?
Start with a big one and spend most of it!

FOSSILS

Newsflash:

Archaeologists have found the **fossils** of a
one-eyed dinosaur; they are going to call it a
Do-you-think-he-saw-us!

FRACTIONS

Who invented **fractions**?
Henry the 1/8th.

FRED

Knock, knock!

Who's there?
Fred.
Fred who?
Fred this needle for me, will you?

FRENCH FRIES

Why are **French fries** so happy?
Because they are chip and cheerful.

FRIDGE

If a **fridge** could sing, would it sing 'Freeze a jolly good fellow'?

FROGS

What's a **frog's** favourite drink?

Croakacola!

Where do **frogs** go to the toilet?
A croakroom!

DOCTOR, DOCTOR, I think I'm a **frog**.
Well, I can't see you now - hop it!

What do you call a girl with a **frog** on her head?
Lily!

What happens if a **frog's** car breaks down?
It gets toad away!

FROGS' LEGS

Man in restaurant: Waiter - do you have **frogs' legs**?
Waiter: No, sir, I've always walked like this!

GAMBLING

What do you call a lady who likes **gambling**?
Betty!

GAME

What **game** do horses like best?
Stable tennis!

GARDENER

Why did the **gardener** plant bulbs?
So that the worms could see where they were going!

WHAT GAVE THE GARDENER HIS LIGHT BULB IDEA?

IT CAME TO HIM IN A FLASH!

GCSE

What do you call a boy with nineteen **GCSEs**?
A liar!

GHERKIN

What did the teacher say to the boy with a
gherkin in each nostril?
'Stop pickle-ing your nose.'

GHOSTS

What is a **ghost's** favourite food?
Spookghetti!
What else?
Ghoulash!

GIRAFFE

What do you get if you cross a **giraffe** witha hedgehog?

A five metre hairbrush!

What do you get if you cross a **giraffe** with an Alsatian dog?
You get an animal that bites low-flying aircraft!

GLASSES

Doctor, Doctor,, I think I need **glasses**.
You certainly do, this is a fish and chip shop!

GLOVE

Did you hear about the cat who swallowed a **glove**?
It had mittens.

GLOW WORMS

What is a **glow worm's** favourite food?
Anything, so long as it's just a light snack!

GNOME

Did you hear about the sick **gnome**?
It went to the elf centre.

GNU

Why was the **gnu** kicked out of the zoo?
For being a gnu-sence.

GOATS

Doctor, Doctor, I think I'm a **goat**!
How long have you felt like this?
Since I was a kid!

GOBLIN

How did the gnome get indigestion?
From goblin his food.

GOLF

Why do people who play **golf** need a spare pair of shoes?
In case they get a hole in one!

What is a **golfer's** favourite snack?
Tees on toast.

GONDOLA

I had my boat stolen in Venice.
What kind of boat is it?
Well as of now, it's a **gone-dola**.

GORILLA

Why do **gorillas** show off?
Because they love the ape-lause.

GRANDFATHER CLOCK

A man was staggering down a road with a huge
grandfather clock on his back. As he turned a
corner the base of it hit a little old lady and nearly
knocked her over.
'*Why can't you wear a wrist-watch like everyone
else!*' she said crossly.

GRANDPA

'Mum, why is **grandpa** wearing two banana skins
on his feet?'
'**He wanted a new pair of slippers!**'

GRANNY

'My **granny** hasn't got a grey hair on her head.'
'**Really?**'
'*Yes, she's completely bald!*'

'My **granny** has teeth like stars.'
'**Really?**'
'*Yes – they come out at night!*'

GRAPE

What did the grape say when the elephant stood on it?

Nothing, it just gave out a little whine!

GRASSHOPPER

Man in restaurant: Waiter, there's a **grasshopper** in my soup!
Waiter: Yes, sir, *it's the fly's day off!*

GREECE

What is the slipperiest country in the world?
***Greece**.*

GREEN

What's **green** and jumps round the garden?
A spring onion!

What's **green** and hairy and goes up and down?
A gooseberry in a lift!

What's **green** and brown and if it jumped out of a tree on to you it would kill you?
A billiard table!

What's **green** and noisy?
A froghorn!

GREY

What's **grey** with four legs and a trunk?
A mouse going on holiday!

What's big and **grey** and has sixteen wheels?
An elephant on roller skates!

A little girl asked her mum why she had some **grey** hairs.
'Probably because you're so naughty to me,' joked her mum.
'You must have been horrible to Granny then!' said the girl.

HAGGIS

Did you hear about the thief who stole a **haggis**?
He got off scot free.

HAIR

DOCTOR, DOCTOR, my **hair** keeps falling out, can
you give me something to keep it in?
Yes, here's a paper bag.

Why did the bald man go outside?
To get some fresh hair!

What kind of **hair** does the sea have?
Wavy.

HAM

Why were slices of **ham** scared of the boiled eggs?
Because they were hard.

HANDS

What can you put in your left **hand** but not
your right?
Your right elbow!

What has **hands** but never washes its face?
A clock!

HANDYMAN

Why has the school caretaker got four arms?
Because he's a **handyman**.

HARMONY

How do musicians get paid?
In **har-money**.

HAT

What did the **hat** say to the tie?
You hang around while I go on ahead!

HEAVEN

What did the police man say when he got to **heaven**?
Halo-ello-ello.

HEDGE

Why did the man grow a **hedge** under his nose?
He wanted a **bushy moustache**.

HEDGEHOG

What's a **hedgehog's** favourite food?
Prickled onions!

HELICOPTER

What flies through the air and stinks?
A **smelly-copter**.

HELMET

Why did the policeman have a sausage on his **helmet**?
He was a member of the frying squad.

HEM

What do you get when a dressmaker gets a tickle in her throat?
A **hem** ahem ahem.

HERB

What's the most popular game in the **herb** garden?
Parsley the parcel.

HOLE

How do mice celebrate when they move to a new **hole**?
With a mouse warming party.

HOLIDAY

How do elephants go on **holiday**?
They travel by jumbo jet!

Where do they go?
Tuskany!

Where do ghosts go for their **holidays**?
The Isle of Fright!

HONEY

Why do bees have sticky hair?
Because they have honey combs.

HORSE

How do you hire a **horse**?
Stand it on four bricks!

HOUSE

A man was asking an estate agent about a **house**
he wanted to buy.
'Does the roof leak?' he asked.
'Only when it rains,' said the agent.

What do you get when an elephant sits on
your **house**?
A flat.

HUMAN CANNON-BALL

Did you hear about the **human cannon-ball** who
lost his job?
They fired him.

HYENA

A **hyena** ate a box of Oxo cubes and made a
laughing stock of itself!

WHAT 'H' WORD IS A MOUNTAIN RANGE WHERE YETIS DO CHOIR PRACTICE?

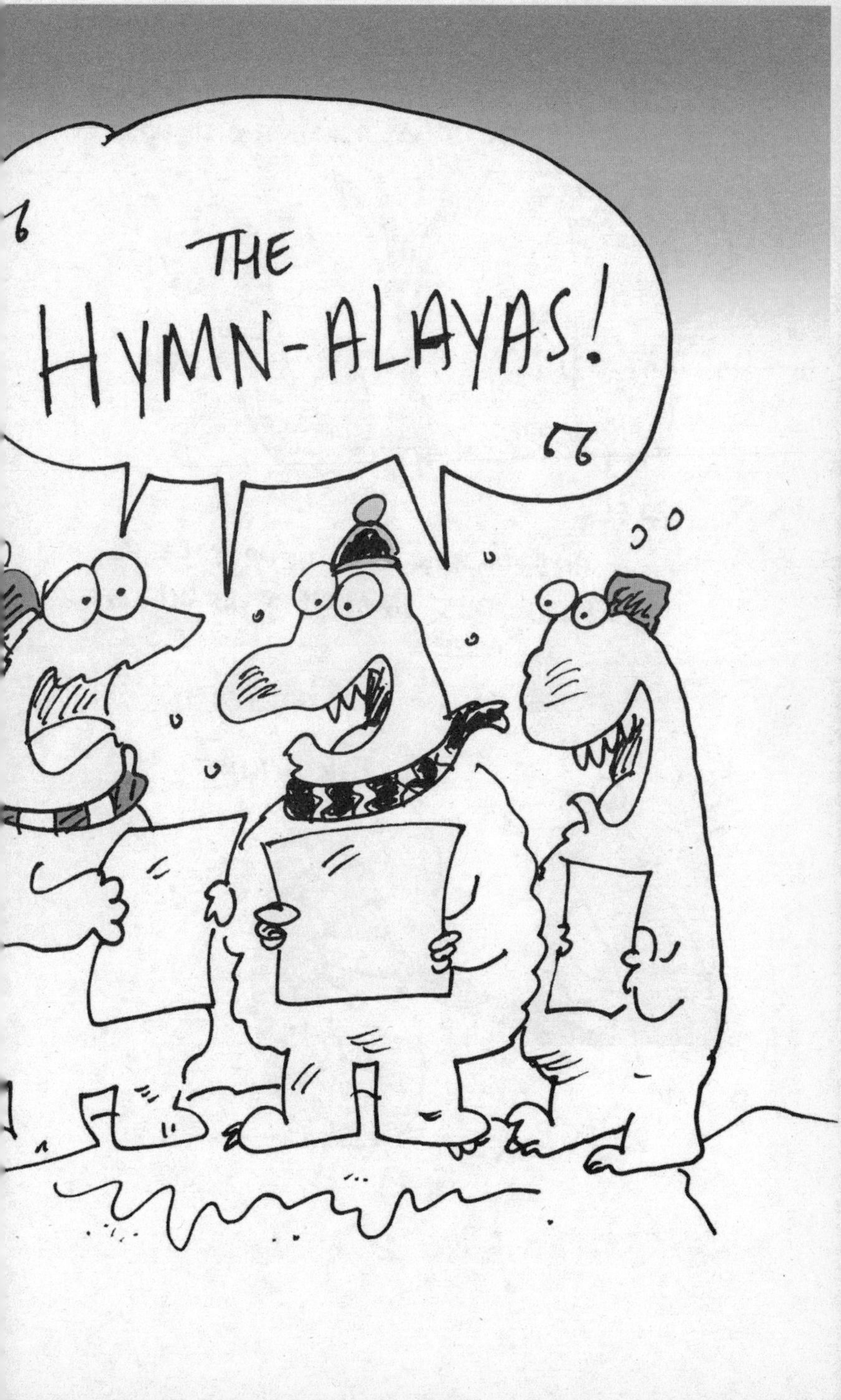
THE
HYMN-ALAYAS!

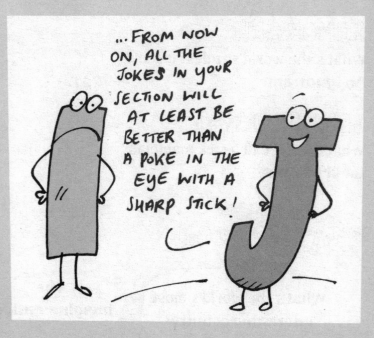

ICE CUBES

What animal do you get when you tie **ice cubes** around your neck?
A chin chiller.

ICE LOLLY

What do snowmen keep in their money boxes?
Ice lolly.

ICICLE

Where do polar bears hang out at school?
Behind the **icicle** sheds.

IGNORANT

What's the world's rudest insect?
An **ignor-ant**.

ILLUSIONIST

What do you call a sick magician?
An **ill-usionist**.

IMAGINATION

What's the world's most interesting country?

The **imagine-nation**.

INDICATOR

A man wanted to know if the **indicator** winkers on his car were working properly so he stopped his car and asked a small boy to look at them and tell him.

'Are they working?' said the man.

'YES NO YES NO YES NO YES NO,' said the boy!

INFLATION

Why do balloons cost so much?

Because of inflation.

INSECT

What do you call an **insect** who is always complaining?

A grumble bee.

IRON

What did one **iron** say to the other iron?

Talk later – I've got a pressing appointment.

ITCH

What's the best way to cope with an **itch**?

Start from scratch.

IVY

Why do ghosts like **ivy**.

Because it's creepy.

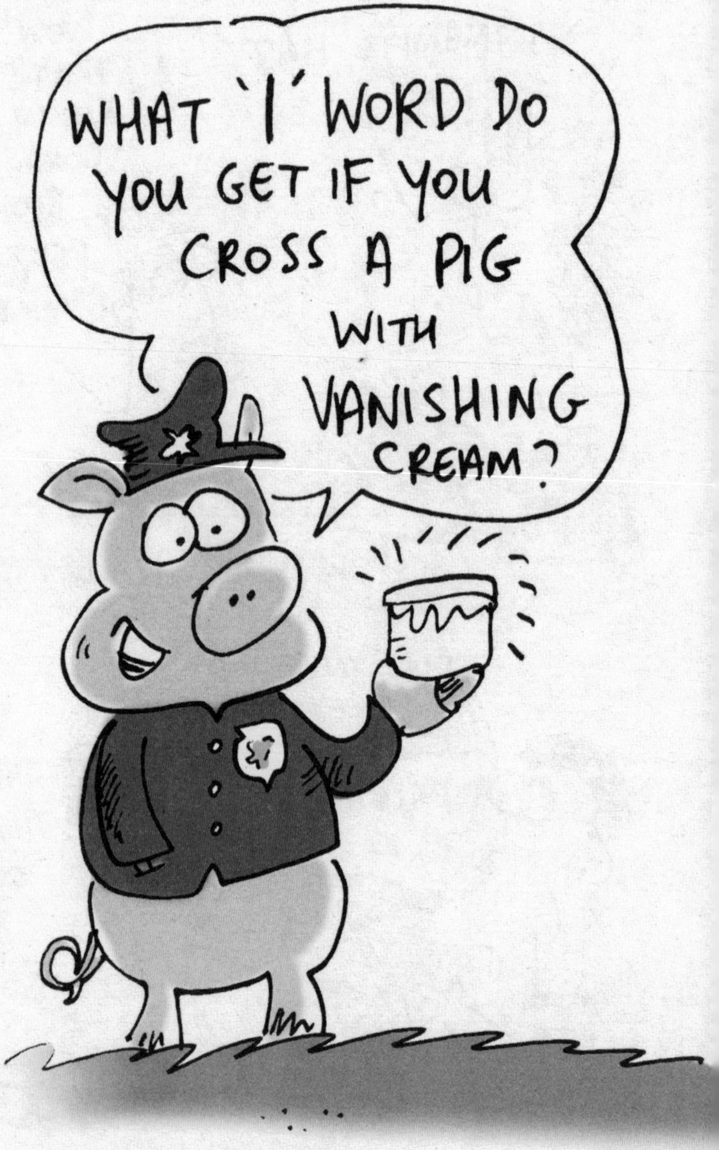
WHAT 'I' WORD DO YOU GET IF YOU CROSS A PIG WITH VANISHING CREAM?

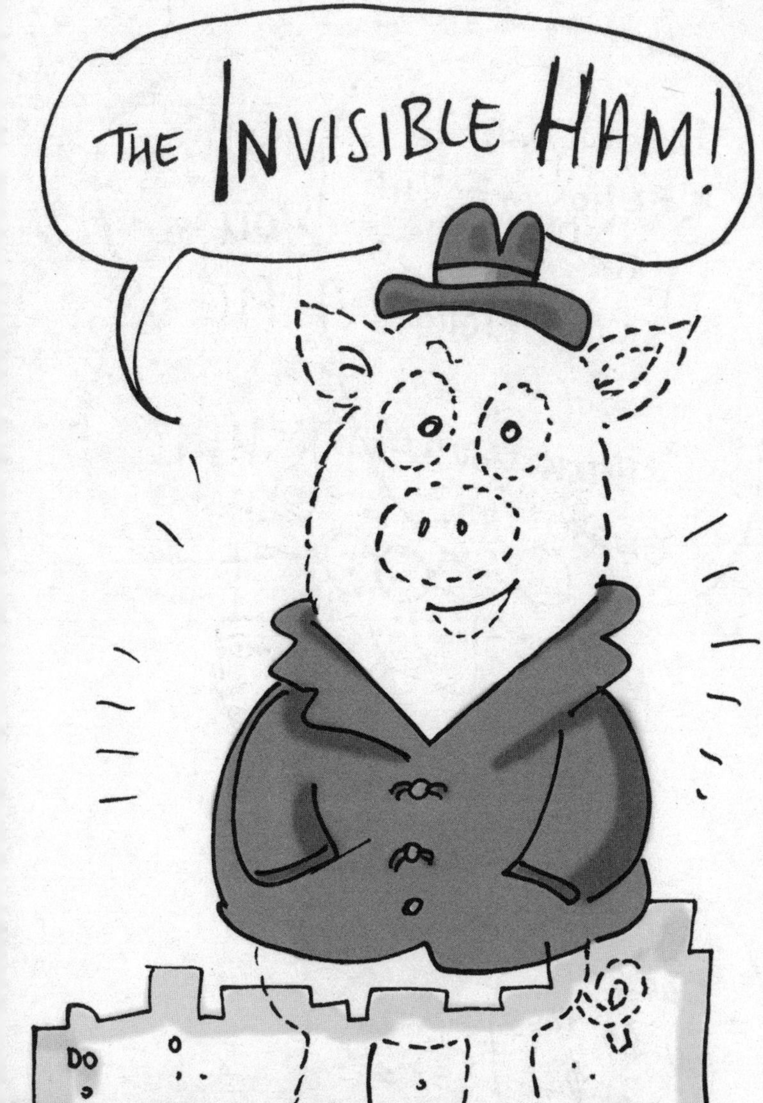
THE INVISIBLE HAM!
DO

JACKET

Why did the man set his **jacket** on fire?
He wanted a blazer.

JAM

What **jam** do traffic wardens like?
Traffic jam.

What's big and grey, sits in a river, and squirts **jam** at you?
A hippopotamus eating a doughnut.

Cookery teacher: Jane, what's the most obvious thing to put into a **jam** sandwich?
Jane: Your teeth!

JAMAICA

Man: My wife is going to the West Indies.
His friend: **Jamaica**?
Man: No, she's going of her own accord!

JEEP

Two men in a jeep were motoring along across the grasslands of Africa. Two lions lay beneath some scrubby bushes near the track ahead of them.
'Look,' said the first lion, 'meals on wheels!'

JELLY

How do you start a **jelly** race?
Get set!

What do you get if you cross a **jelly** with a sheep dog?
Colliewobbles!

A man was sitting on a park bench with a **jelly** in one ear and some fruit in the other. A boy went up to him and said: 'Excuse me, but you've got a jelly in one ear and some fruit in the other.' *'You'll have to speak up,'* said the man. *'I'm a trifle deaf.'*

JELLYFISH
What did one **jellyfish** say to the other jellyfish?
Stings ain't what they used to be.

JESTER
Who tells the world's fastest jokes?
Jester Minute.

JEWELLER
What's the difference between a **jeweller** and a jailer?
One sells watches, the other watches cells!

JOG
What's spiky and wears a tracksuit?
A hedge-jog.

JOHN
What did St **John** say when he tried to teach St Luke road safety?
Stop, Luke, and listen!

JOKES

Have you heard the **joke** about the brick wall?
No.
I won't tell it to you, you'd never get over it!

Have you heard the **joke** about the quick sand?
No.
It will take a long time to sink in.

Do you know the **joke** about chicken-pox?
No.
I won't tell it to you, you'd only go and pass it on!

Do you know the **joke** about the broken pencil?
No.
I won't tell it to you, there's no point to it!

Knock knock!

Who's there?
Boo.
Boo who?
There's no need to cry, it's only a joke!

I know a **joke** about butter, but I'm not going to spread it!

I know a **joke** about a dustbin, but it's absolute rubbish!

JUDGE

What do you call a **judge** who does conjuring tricks?
A magic-strate.

JUICE

Why is fresh orange **juice** no good at computer games?
It lacks concentration.

JUNGLE

Why shouldn't you play cards in the **jungle**?
There are too many cheetahs!

What's white and fluffy and swings through the **jungle**?

A meringue-ootang.

What do you call a polar bear in a **jungle**?
Lost!

JUNO

Knock Knock!

Who's there?
Juno.
Juno who?
Juno how long I've been waiting for you to open this door?

KANGAROO

What do you get if you cross a sheep with a **kangaroo**?
A woolly jumper!

What do you give a **kangaroo** for dinner?
Jumping beans.

What do you call a baby **kangaroo** who sits in front of the TV?
A pouch potato.

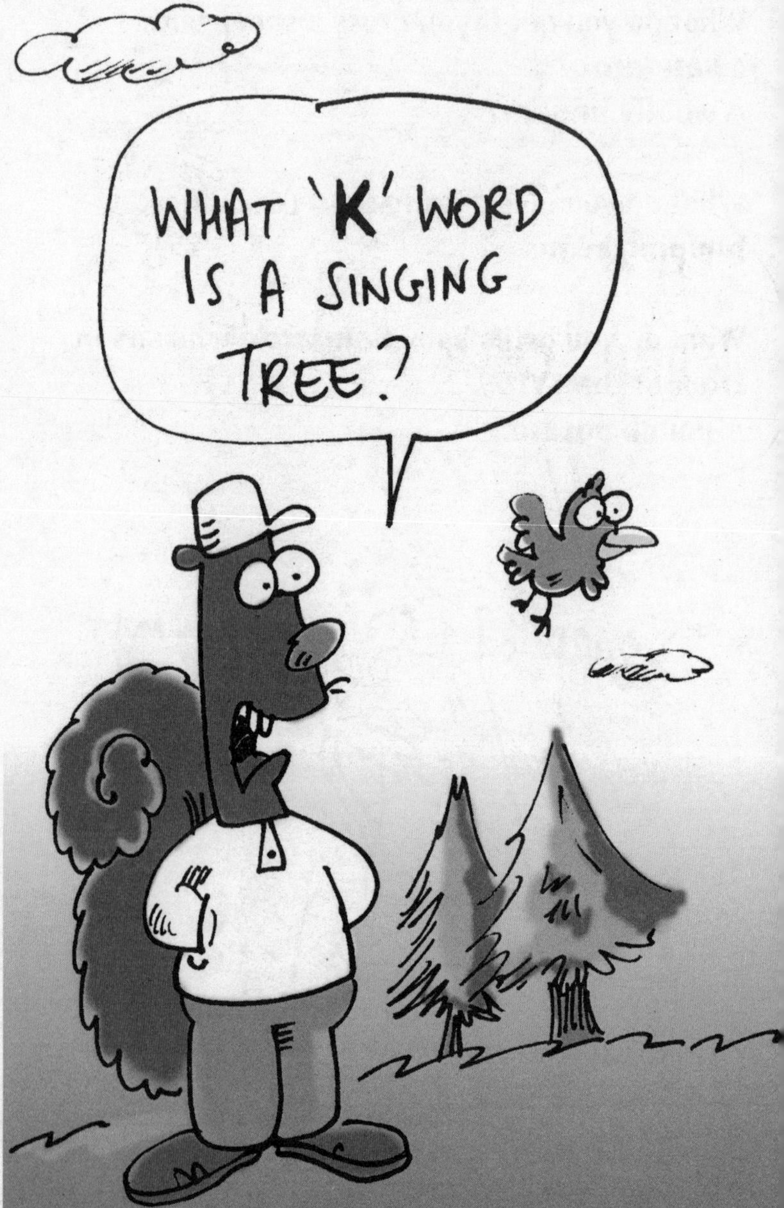
WHAT 'K' WORD IS A SINGING TREE?

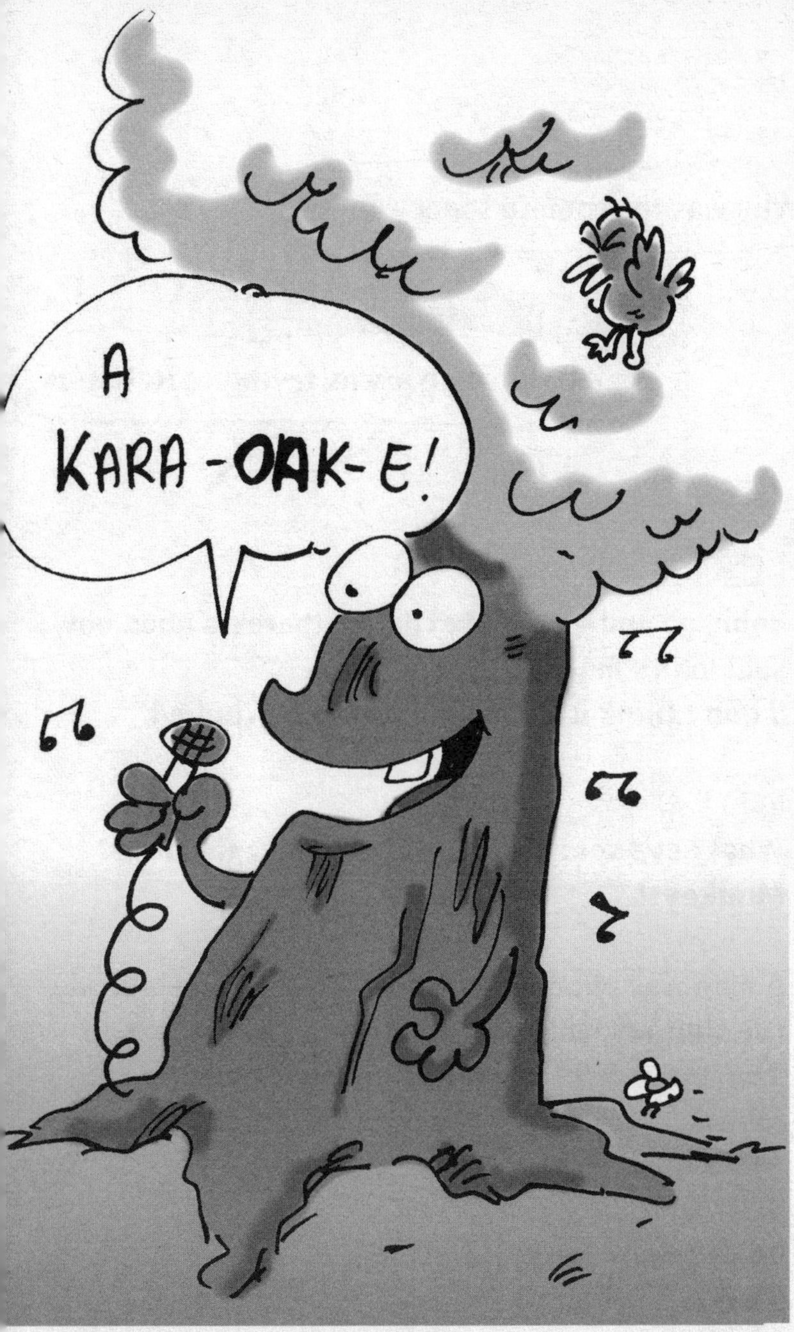
A KARA-OAK-E!

KETCHUP

Why was the tomato sauce runny?

Because it was trying to **ketchup**.

KETTLE

'John, go and put the **kettle** on, there's a good boy,' said John's mother.
'I don't think it will fit me, Mum,' he replied.

KEYS

What **keys** scratch themselves under the arms?
Monkeys!

A man was phoning a garage: 'Please come quickly, I've shut my keys in my sports car,' said the man. 'Hurry, I've left the roof open and it's starting to rain.'

KHAKI

What colour can start an engine?
Khaki.

KID

What do baby goats wear in winter?
Kid gloves.

KING

Where does the **king** keep his armies?
Up his sleevies!

Who succeeded the first **king** of England?
The second one.

KIPPER

Who is the most important player on the undersea
football team?
The goal kipper.

KNAPSACK

What sits on your back and snores?
A napsack.

KNEES

Knock! Knock!

'Who's there?'
'Isn't **knees**.'
'Isn't knees who?'
'Isn't **kneasy waiting out here for you to open
the door**.'

KNEAD

What did the baker say to the dough?
You're all **I knead** to get by.

KNIFE

What do you call a man with a **knife** on his head?
Stanley!

KNIGHTS

Where do **knights** learn how to fight?

At knight school of course!

What is a **knight's** favourite Christmas carol?
Silent knight!

KNITTING

A lady was driving very fast down the road in a sports car. A policeman watched her go past and noticed that as well as driving she was **knitting**. He leapt on to his motorbike and chased her. When he got alongside her car he leant over and said, 'Pull over.'
'No,' shouted back the lady. 'A scarf!'

KNOCK KNOCK!

Knock Knock!

Who's there?
Tish.
Tish who?
Bless you!

Knock Knock!

Who's there?
Twitter.
Twitter who?
I didn't know you did owl impressions!

Knock Knock!

Who's there?
Micky.
Micky who?
Micky won't fit, that's why I'm knocking!

Knock Knock!

Who's there?
Isabel.
Isabel who?
Isabel not better than all this silly knocking?

Knock knock!

Who's there?
Doctor.
Doctor who?
That's right!

Knock, knock

Who's there?
My dose.
Mydose who?
My dose is duck id your ledderbox.

KOALA

What's the most popular drink in Australia?

Coca **Koala**.

KUNG FU

What disease do martial artists get?
Kung flu.

LABORATORY
FOR SALE!

DR BORIS VON BARKING, MAD
SCIENTIST IS OFFERING HIS OWN
LABORATORY — THE VERY ONE IN
WHICH HE CREATED HIS **NEW GIANT
MONSTER** — FOR QUICK SALE!

(UNFORTUNATELY ALTHOUGH HE BROUGHT THE
MONSTER TO LIFE, HE DIDN'T HAVE TIME TO
TEACH HIM THE DIFFERENCE BETWEEN
'LABORATORY' AND 'LAVATORY' SO IF YOU BUY
IT YOU MAY FIND IT A BIT...ER... WATERLOGGED).

LABRADOR

Fascinating fact ➤ If you cross a **labrador** with a tortoise, you get an animal that goes to the newsagent's and comes back with last week's paper.

LADDER

Did you hear about the man who fell off a sixty-foot **ladder**?
He wasn't hurt though - he was only on the second rung!

LAKE

First man: I wonder if this **lake** is very deep?
Second man: It can't be, it doesn't come up very far on the ducks.

LAMB CHOPS

Lady: Two nice **lamb chops** please: make them lean.
Butcher: *Certainly, madam, which way?*

LAMP

Where do ghosts keep their **lamps**?
On their deadside tables.

LANDING

What's that aeroplane doing at the top of our stairs?
Someone must have left the **landing** light on!

ROLL UP! ROLL UP! IT'S ONLY FITTING WE CONTINUE OUR 'L' SECTION WITH THE
BIGGEST LAUGH
IN THE BOOK!

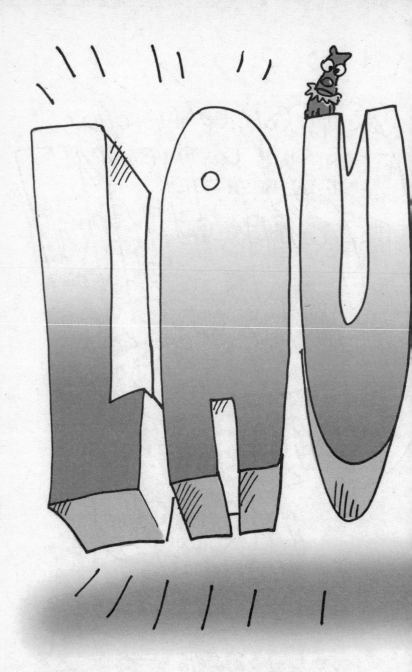

LAVATORIES

What do you call a lady with two **lavatories**?
Lou Lou!

LAWYER

What's a good first name for a **lawyer**?
Sue.

LEAVES

What do you call a man who walks through
autumn **leaves**?
Russell!

LEAPFROG

What's green and comes out on February 29th?
A leapfrog.

LEGS

What has fifty **legs** and can't walk?

Half a centipede!

What do you call a lady with one **leg** shorter than
the other?
I lean!

LEMONADE

When is **lemonade** like a bandage?
When you use it for thirst aid!

LEOPARDS

Fascinating fact ➯ **Leopards** who try to escape from zoos are always spotted.

LETTERBOX

What do you call a man who comes through your **letterbox** in the morning?
Bill!

LETTUCE

Knock Knock!

Who's there?
Lettuce.
Lettuce who?
Lettuce in, there's a good fellow!

LIBRARIAN

A frog went into a library. The **librarian**, trying to be kind, offered it all sorts of books to read. But the sulky frog didn't want any of them - it just sat there saying '**reddit, reddit, reddit.**'

LICE

Teacher: Where do **lice** live?
Boy: **Search me**.
Teacher: No, thanks!

LIES

What do you call an alien who **lies**?
An Unidentified Fibbing Object.

LIFT

What did one **lift** say to the other?
I think I'm coming down with something.

LIGHTS

A policeman stopped a motorist. 'Excuse me, sir, your back **lights** aren't working.'
The driver got out of the car to look. Then he started to howl with despair, and tear his hair, and make a terrible scene.
'Hang on, sir,' said the officer. 'I haven't arrested you or anything - I was just pointing out that your back lights aren't working.'
'Never mind my back lights,' screamed the man. 'Where's my caravan!'

LION

Lion: You're a cheater!
Cheetah: You're lion!

Why do **lions** paint their toe-nails green?
So they can hide in a cabbage patch!
What nonsense!
Have you ever seen a lion in a cabbage patch?
No
There you are - it works!

LIPS

Why do we have **lips**?
To stop our mouths fraying at the edges.

LITTLE OLD LADY

Knock knock!

Who's there?
Little old lady.
Little old lady who?
I didn't know you could yodel!

LOLLYPOP

What has a sweet taste and flies?
A **lollipop** left out in the garden.

LORRY

Newsflash: A **lorry** load of glue was spilt on the motorway today - police have asked drivers to stick to their own lanes.

A **lorry** loaded with hair restorer overturned. Police had to comb the area.

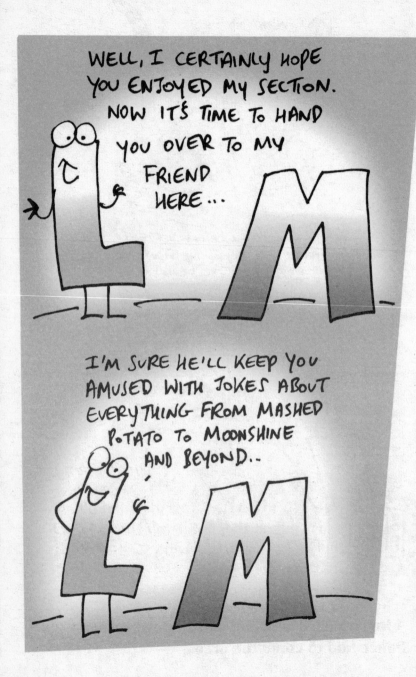

MAGGOT

What's worse than finding a **maggot** in your apple?
Finding half a maggot in your apple!

MAGICAL

Who is the most **magical** secret agent?
James Wand.

MAGNA CARTA

Teacher: Where was the **Magna Carta** signed?
Boy: **At the bottom!**

MANNERS

Why do bees have such good **manners**?
Because they always beehive themselves.

MAY DAY

A pilot was flying happily along when suddenly one
of his engines caught fire.
'**May Day**, May Day,' he shouted into his radio.
'This is the control tower,' said the voice on the
radio. 'Please state your height and position.'
'I'm about five foot eleven inches, and I'm sitting
down,' replied the pilot.

What do you call a snowman on **May Day**?

A puddle.

MEDICINE

A man wasn't feeling very well so he went to see the doctor. The doctor took a look at him, made some notes, and gave him a bottle of **medicine**. 'Right,' he said. 'I want you to go home and drink this medicine, followed by a nice hot bath: come back and see me next week.' The man went back a week later.

'How did you get on?' asked the doctor kindly.
'Well,' said the man. 'I managed to take the medicine, but I didn't manage to drink all the bath...'

MEMORY

DOCTOR, DOCTOR, I've lost my **memory**.
When did it happen?
When did what happen?

Boy (to teacher): I've got a very good **memory**, Miss – in fact I've got a photographic mind!
Teacher: It's a pity it hasn't been developed...

MILK

Will you join me in a glass of milk?
OK, you get in first.

MILKSHAKE

How do you make a really good **milkshake**?
Tell it a scary story.

MILLIONAIRE

Rich man: My wife has turned me into
a **millionaire**.
His friend: Really?
Rich man: Yes, before I met her I was
a multimillionaire!

MIND

A little girl went to her mother and said:
'Mummy, I've changed my **mind**.'
'Does the new one work any better?' replied her
mother.

MINI

What time is it when an elephant sits on your
Mini?
Time to get a new Mini!

MIRROR

A little girl's mother went into her daughter's bedroom and found her standing in front of a mirror with her eyes closed.

'Whatever are you doing, dear?' she asked.

'I'm trying to see what I look like when I'm asleep!' **said the girl**.

MONEY

A doctor asked a nurse how the boy who had swallowed some **money** was getting on.

'No change yet,' said the nurse!

Fascinating fact ➡ **Money** doesn't grow on trees, though banks have many branches.

MONKEY

What **monkey** looks like a flower?

A chimp-pansy.

WHAT'S THE ABOMINABLE SNOWMAN'S FAVOURITE ITALIAN MEAL?
SPAGH-YETI!

WHAT'S HAIRY AND BOUNDS ROUND TRANSYLVANIA SHOUTING OUT RUDE WORDS?
CENSORED!
A SWEAR-WOLF!

MONSTERS

What do sea **monsters** like to eat?

Fish and ships!

MOON

Have you heard about the two men who opened up a restaurant on the **moon**?
The food was very good, but the place lacked atmosphere!

MOTHER

First boy: My **mother** does bird impressions.
Second boy: Really?
First boy: Yes, she watches me like a hawk!

'I can't hear a word my **mother** says.'
'Why's that?'
'She always mum-bles.'

MOTORBIKE

Did you hear about the boy who thought that his dad had a magic **motorbike**? He'd heard his mother saying that she'd heard it turning into their drive!

NEED THE ULTIMATE
MOUSE
TRAP?

IF YOUR HOUSE IS OVERRUN WITH MICE DON'T DESPAIR! OUR PROMISE IS TO RID YOUR HOUSE OF MICE ONCE AND FOR ALL AND WE DON'T EVEN WANT YOUR MONEY!

(HOW IS THIS SPECIAL DEAL POSSIBLE? EASY — SINCE WE GET RID OF THE MICE BY STUFFING SIX LARGE SNAKES THROUGH YOUR LETTERBOX, WE'LL SIMPLY TAKE YOUR HOUSE AS PAYMENT AFTER YOU'VE ABANDONED IT.)

MOUSE

How do you help a drowning **mouse**?

Give it mouse to mouse resuscitation!

Why can't you get milk from a **mouse**?
You can't get a bucket under a mouse!

MOUSETRAP

Spell **mousetrap** using only three letters.
C A T.

'I'd like a **mousetrap**, and please hurry up, I've got a bus to catch.'
'Sorry, madam. We haven't got any that big.'

MUSICAL

What is the most **musical** fish?

A piano tuna!

TEST YOUR J.Q....

Why did MOZART compose his tunes in Bed?

Because he wanted to write Sheet MUSIC.

NAG

Mum: Do you think I **nag**?
Son: No . . . but can you please stop going on about it?

NAILS

Two men were standing on scaffolding, knocking **nails** into the walls of a house. One of the men kept tossing nails over his shoulder on to the ground. 'Why do you keep throwing nails away?' asked the other.
'They've got points at the wrong end,' said the man.
'Don't be an idiot!' scolded his mate. 'We can use them on the other side of the house!'

Do you file your **nails**?
No, I cut them off and throw them away.

NAKED

Why did the nudist buy a lie detector?
To find out the **naked** truth.

NAVEL

How do you close up your **navel**?
With a belly button.

NET

A **net** is just a lot of holes tied together with string.

NETTLE

Did you hear the joke about the **nettles**?
Yes, but I couldn't quite grasp it.

NEWSPAPER

What's in the **newspaper** on Friday nights?
Fish and chips!

NIGHTINGALE

What's scary and sings like a bird?

A **nightin-ghoul**.

NOAH

Knock knock!
Who's there?
Noah.
Noah who?
Noah any more knock knock jokes?

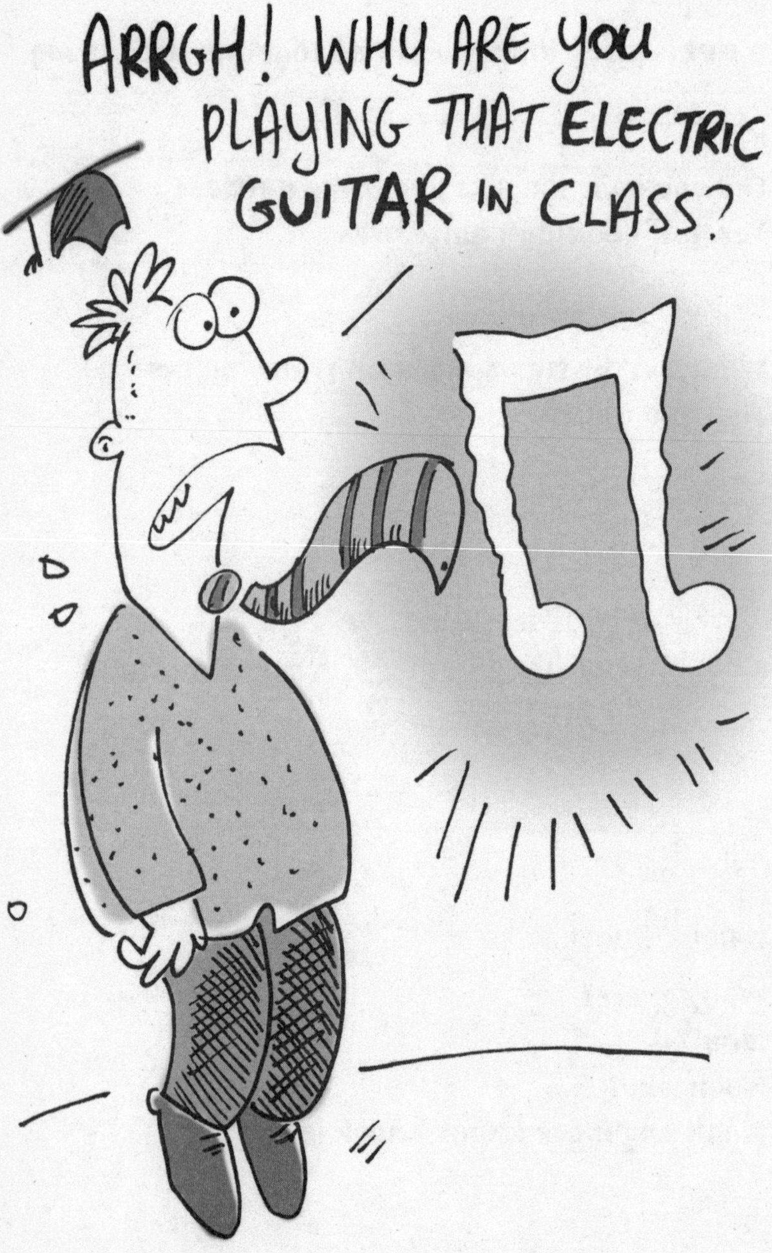
ARRGH! WHY ARE YOU PLAYING THAT ELECTRIC GUITAR IN CLASS?

NOTICE

A man walked into a police station and told the officer that he had lost his dog.

'Have you tried putting a **notice** in your local shops, sir?' asked the policeman.

'That wouldn't do any good,' replied the man. *'My dog can't read!'*

NOTICEBOARD

Where do you hang really uninteresting messages?
On the **notice-bored**.

NUMB

What keeps the rain off and has no feelings?
A **numb**-rella.

NUMBER

Why is the **number** six scared of the number seven?
Because seven eight nine.

A man made a telephone call.

'Hello,' he said. 'Is that 3764?'

'No,' said the voice on the other end. '**You must have a wrong number**.'

'If it's a wrong number, why did you answer the phone?' said the man.

An absent-minded professor's phone rang in the middle of the night.

'Hello,' he said. 'Professor Nutter's phone.'

'I'm sorry,' said a voice on the phone. 'I must have a wrong **number**.'

'That's all right,' said the professor. 'I had to get up anyway to answer the phone.'

NURSE

Doctor: Have you taken this patient's pulse, **Nurse**?

Nurse: No, is it missing?

Why did the **nurse** tiptoe past the medicine cabinet?

She didn't want to wake the sleeping pills!

NUTCRACKERS

What do nuts have at Christmas?

Nutcrackers.

OCEAN

Why does the **ocean** roar?
So would you if you had crabs walking round on your bottom!

OCTOPUS

Never attack an **octopus** – they're always well armed.

OFF!

Man in pub: Well, I'm **off**.
Other drinker: I wondered what the smell was…

OLD

A very **old** man was celebrating his birthday at an old people's home. A young interviewer from the local paper came to ask him questions:
'How do you account for the fact that you've lived so long?' she asked.
'I reckon it's because I was born such a long time ago,' said the man.

'She's so **old**, she was born in 1956.'
'That's not old.'
'1956 BC.'

OLDEN DAYS

Boy: I wished I'd lived in the **olden days**, Mum.
Mother: Why?
Boy: I wouldn't have to do history lessons!

ONE-WAY STREET

Policeman: Excuse me, sir, are you aware that this
is a **one-way street**?
Man: But officer - I was only going one way!

ONION

Why is an **onion** like a bell?
They can both be peeled.

OPTICIAN

They're building an **optician's** shop next to
our school.
It's a site for sore eyes.

ORANGE

What's **orange** and sounds like a parrot?
A carrot!

Why did the **orange** sit down in the middle of
the road?
It wanted to play a game of squash with
the cars!

TEST YOUR J.Q.
WHY did the MonKey Lie on the SUNBED?

TO GET AN ORANGU-TAN!

YES, THERE HE IS FOLKS- MEET ORVILLE O. OLIPHANT FROM 'ORVILLE'S OSCAR COURIERS' HE'S THE GUY WHO PICKS UP THE STATUES FROM THE FACTORY AND BRINGS THEM TO THE AWARDS CEREMONY..

OSTRICHES

Did you ever see an **ostrich** fly?
No, they make sure they're properly zipped up.

Why do **ostriches** make good steaks?
Because they all go to cookery classes.

OWLS

Did you hear about the man who crossed an **owl** with a skunk?
He got a bird that smelled terrible but didn't give a hoot!

Why did the **owl** 'owl?
Because the woodpecker would pecker!

PHEW! ANYONE WHO WONDERS WHY OSTRICHES STICK THEIR HEADS IN THE SAND — HASN'T SMELLED THAT STINKY OWL!

PUBLISHER! PRAY TELL
WHY THIS PESKY
PIECE OF PLASTIC
IS ON MY
POUFFE?

BECAUSE WE
DIDN'T WANT
A POEM—WE
WANTED A
FAIRY TALE...

PREPOSTEROUS! WHAT
PIDDLING PARABLE
COULD YOU POSSIBLY
PREFER TO MY POETRY?

THE ONE
YOU'RE PART OF:
"THE PRINCESS
AND THE P"

PAINTING

> What do you get if you cross music and **painting**?

> Notz-art.

PANCAKE

'Waiter, I'm in a hurry, will my **pancake** be long?'
'No, sir. It'll be round and flat.'

PANDA

> What do you get if you cross a **panda** with a harmonium?

> Pandamonium!

PANDA CAR

A policeman who drove a **panda car** went to see his mother. He rang the door bell.
'Who is it?' called his mum.
'*It's meema meema meema*,' said the panda car driver.

READ ALL ABOUT IT! LATEST JOKES IN THE PAPERS

PAPER SHOP

A man was looking very down in the dumps.
'What's the matter, Jack?' asked a friend.
'It's terrible,' replied Jack. 'I've just lost all my life's savings.'
'How did it happen?'
'Well,' said Jack sadly, 'I bought a **paper shop**, and it blew away...'

PARIS

Fascinating fact The food is delicious in **Paris**, especially the Trifle Tower.

PARK

Where do you **park** a spaceship?

At a parking meteor.

PARROT

Teacher: If you had a **parrot**, Mary, what would you feed it on?
Mary: Pollyfiller, Miss!

What do you get if you cross a **parrot** with an elephant?
An animal that tells you all it can remember!

PARSNIPS

What do you call a man with a **parsnip** stuck in each ear?
Anything - he can't hear you!

PEDESTRIAN

A **pedestrian** was trying to cross a very busy main road. A policeman came up to him.
'There's a zebra crossing just up the road, sir,' he said.
'Well,' said the man, *'I hope he's having better luck than I am!'*

PETROL

What's a good first name for a **petrol** station attendant?
Phil.

PELICAN

Fascinating fact ➤ It's very expensive to keep **pelicans**, you could face some very large bills.

PERFUME

Why do vicars wear the nicest **perfume**?
Because it's heaven scent.

PHONE

School boy: Billy is too ill to come to school today.
Teacher: Who is that speaking?
School boy: My dad!

PIANO

Do you know why pianos are so difficult to open?
Because they've got dozens of keys and they're
all on the inside!

Why did the piano laugh?
Because someone was tickling the ivories.

PICK YOUR OWN

200

PIGS

What do you give a sick **pig**?
Oinkment!

What do you get if you cross a **pig** with itching powder?
Pork scratchings!

PIGEONS

What do you get if you cross a parrot with a homing **pigeon**?
A bird that asks the way home!

PIGLETS

Why don't **piglets** listen to their fathers?
Because they are boars!

PILLS

What **pills** do you give to an elephant that can't sleep?
Trunkquillizers!

'Doctor, it says here, "Take one **pill** four times a day."'
'So – what's the problem?'
'I can't tell which pill I have to keep taking from the rest of them!'

PLANT

What do you get if you **plant** jokes?
A corn field.

POCKETS

Maths teacher: Michael, if you had six pounds in one **pocket**, and seven pounds in Another pocket, and three pounds in your back pocket, what would you have?
Michael: Someone else's trousers on!

POLAR BEARS

What do **polar bears** have for lunch?
Iceburgers!

POLICEMAN

A **policeman** saw a tortoise walking up the motorway. He screeched up to it in his police car.
'What do you think you're doing on the motorway?' he asked the poor animal.
'About two metres an hour,' said the tortoise.

A **policeman** could live at: 999, Letsby Avenue.

What did the three-headed **policeman** say?
'Hello, Hello, Hello!'

POLYGON

Teacher: What's a **polygon**?
Girl: An empty parrot cage, Miss!

POP

What do **pop** singers get from too much dancing?
Pop-corns.

POSTMAN PAT

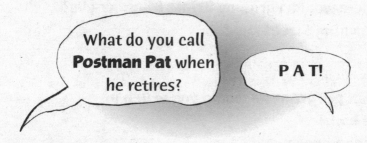

What do you call **Postman Pat** when he retires?

P A T!

PRAYER

Mother: Have you said your prayers tonight?
Girl: Yes, I prayed that God would make four and four make nine.
Mother: Why?
Girl: Because that's what I put in my maths test.

PRESENT

Where do you find a Christmas **present** for your cat?
In a catalogue.

PRICKLY

What's green and **prickly**?
A seasick hedgehog!

PRICKLY PEAR

Teacher: What's a **prickly pear**?
Boy: Two hedgehogs!

PRIME MINISTER

Where would a grumpy **Prime Minister** live?
Frowning Street.

PROGRAMME

What **programme** would you watch in
the bath?
A soap opera.

PRONUNCIATION

What word is always **pronounced** wrongly?
Wrongly!

PRUNES

Why did the **prune**
go out with a fig?

He couldn't
get a date.

PSYCHOLOGIST

DOCTOR, DOCTOR, I keep seeing green hairy monsters with hideous faces!
Have you seen a psychologist?
No, just green hairy monsters with hideous faces!

PUB

None of the **pubs** round here want to serve my dad. But then, who'd want to buy him?

PUPPY

A small boy asked his mother if he could have a **puppy** for Christmas.
'No,' she replied. 'You'll have turkey like everybody else.'

PURPLE

What's **purple** with yellow spots and hairy legs and a poisonous sting and great big feelers?
I don't know.
Neither do I, but one's just gone down your neck!

PYJAMAS

Boastful man: When I was big game hunting once, I shot a tiger in my **pyjamas**.
Bored lady: What was a tiger doing wearing your pyjamas?

DOCTOR QUACK'S QUERIES...

YOUR HEALTH IS NO JOKE. WELL, ACTUALLY, ON THIS PAGE IT *IS*!

QUALITY

How do you tell if a hedge is of good **quality**?
Check it with a thicket inspector.

QUARREL

What do chefs hit each other with when they
quarrel?
Spat-ulas.

QUARRY

Why do **quarry** workers often fall out?
They have a very rocky relationship.

QUASIMODO'S PARISIAN PUNCHLINES!

IT IS I, QUASIMODO – NUMBER ONE BELLRINGER IN PARIS! HERE'S MY COLLECTION OF FAB FRENCH FUNNIES! IF YOU CAN THINK OF BETTER ONES, PLEASE GIVE ME A RING!

QUEASY

What do you sing to a sick person on his birthday?
'For **queasy** jolly good fellow.'

QUEEN

Why does the **Queen** do the birthday honours in the morning?
Because she likes an early knight.

QUESTION

Why did you burst that balloon in your fiancee's ear?

I wanted to pop the **question**.

QUESTION MARK

Why did the **question mark** have a safety pin in its nose?
So it could be used for punk-tuation.

QUEUE

Why is everyone standing at that bus stop dressed in a woolly top?
Those are their **queue** jumpers.

QUICHE

What did one **quiche** say to the other quiche?

I'm one of your biggest flans.

QUIET

Who was the **quietest** person at the Round Table?
The silent knight.

QUILL

Why did Shakespeare write so many plays?
Just to quill some time.

QUIT

Why did the new store Santa **quit** on his first day?
He'd heard they were planning to give him the sack.

QUIVER

Why did Robin Hood stick his arrows in jelly?
He was told you had to keep them in a quiver.

QUOTE

Where do writers keep their favourite sayings?

On a **quote** hanger.

RABBIT

What do you call a man with a **rabbit** up his jumper?

Warren!

What do you get if you pour boiling water down a **rabbit** hole?
Hot, cross **bunnies**!

RAIN

How do we know **rain** is tough?
It's always falling to earth without getting hurt.

RASBERRY JAM

Why is **raspberry jam** red?

To see what's on the label.

CURE YOUR ACHING FUNNYBONE WITH THESE REMARKABLE

REMEDIES!

HOW DO YOU CURE WATER ON THE BRAIN?

WITH A TAP ON THE HEAD!

HOW DO I STOP MY NOSE RUNNING?

HIDE IT'S TRAINERS!

REPTILES

Which **reptiles** are good at arithmetic?
Adders!

HOW DO WIND-UP REPTILES OPERATE?

LIKE CROCK-WORK!

REQUESTS

A man was having a meal in a very posh hotel.
'Waiter,' he said. 'Does the band do **requests**?'
'Yes, sir.'
'Good - ask them to go and play outside!'

RESTAURANT

A **restaurant** claimed to cook anything a
customer wanted, so an annoying man went
in and sat down and asked for a rhinoceros
omelette and chips. 'Certainly, sir,' said the
waiter and he went off to the kitchen. A few
minutes later he returned and whispered to the
annoying man, *'I'm sorry, sir, we seem to have run
out of potatoes.'*

Man in restaurant: How long have you worked here?
Waitress: Two months.
Man: Oh, well it can't have been you who took my order…

A lion went into a **restaurant** and sat down.
The waiter went over to it: 'What would you like to eat, sir?' he asked.
'**You**,' said the lion, *licking his lips!*

RHINOCEROS
What steps would you take if you were being pursued by a mad **rhinoceros**?
Very big ones!

RICE
Why did the chef burn his feet while cooking a tin of **rice**?
The label said 'Stand in boiling water for half an hour'.

RICE PUDDING
Why does **rice** pudding get stuck in traffic?
Because it always gets mixed up in the jam.

RIVER

What do you call a girl who stands with one leg on each side of a **river**?
Bridget!

And what do you call a man who swims in slow circles in a **river**?
Eddy!

ROAD

Why did the hedgehog cross the **road**?
To see his flat mate!

Why *didn't* the skeleton cross the **road**?
He didn't have the guts!

ROBBER

First man: Did you hear about the **robber** who went into a bank and was arrested?
Second man: No.
First man: It was full of coppers!

What do you call two **robbers**?
A pair of nickers!

ROBIN HOOD

How did **Robin Hood** tie his shoelaces?
With a long bow.

WHY DID THE TEACHER BAN SPANNERS FROM THE ROBOT SCHOOL CANTEEN?

TO STOP THE PUPILS BOLTING THEIR FOOD.

WHICH ROBOT DIDN'T GO TO THE BALL?

TIN-DERELLA.

ROLLS-ROYCE

A man set his heart on buying a **Rolls-Royce**. For years and years he saved every penny he could, until finally he had enough money to buy one. He went to the car showroom and selected the one he wanted. When the salesman asked for the money – a gigantic sum – the man turned out his pockets and put all his money on the car salesman's desk. The salesman counted it. 'I'm sorry, sir,' he said. 'But you're four pence short of the price.'

'Don't worry,' said the excited buyer, and he rushed out into the street and went up to a newspaper seller.

'Excuse me, mate,' he said. 'Could you spare me four pence? I want to buy a Rolls-Royce.'

'That's OK,' said the newspaper seller. 'Here's eight pence – get one for me too!'

ROMAN

Who cut the **Roman** Empire in half?
A pair of Caesars.

ROSE

A boy came to school with a great big red swelling on the end of his nose.

'How did you get that?' asked a teacher.

'I was smelling a brose,' said the boy sadly.

'I think you mean ROSE,' replied the teacher. 'There's no "B" in rose.'

'There was in this one!' said the boy.

SSSSSSSSSSSSSSSSSSS
LOOK I THINK EVERYONE KNOWS HOW TO MAKE THE 'S' SOUND. I KNOW YOURS IS THE NEXT SECTION OF THE BOOK, BUT YOU DON'T NEED TO GO ON AND ON ABOUT IT...

I'M NOT GOING ON ABOUT IT- I'VE GOT A PUNCTURE! ENJOY THESE 'S' JOKES- I'M OFF TO FIND A BICYCLE PUMP!
SSSSSSSS

SANTA CLAUS'S WIFE

What do you call **Mrs Santa Claus**?
Mary Christmas, of course!

SAUSAGE ROLL

How do you make a **sausage roll**?
Push it down a hill.

SAUSAGES

Sausages are rude – they spit.

SCHOOL

What do ducks bring to **school** in their lunchboxes?
Cream quackers.

SEA

What lies at the bottom of the sea and shakes?
A nervous wreck!

Which **sea** creature goes to the toilet eight times
in one day?
An octopoos.

SEAGULL

A man went into a doctor's surgery with a large
white **seagull** on the top of his head.
'What seems to be the trouble?' asked the doctor.
'*Well*,' said the seagull, '*I've got this man stuck to
my feet!*'

What do you call a man with a **seagull** on his head?
Cliff!

Two not very bright gentlemen were walking along the beach.
'Look,' said one of them suddenly. 'A dead **seagull**!'
'Where?' said his friend, looking up in the sky.

SEASICK
What do you give a **seasick** gorilla?
Plenty of room!

SHAKESPEARE
Teacher: What did **Shakespeare** use to write with?
Boy: A pencil - either a 2B or not 2B.

SHARKS
Why is it easy to fool a **shark**?
They'll swallow anything!

Boy: Have you ever seen a man-eating **shark**?
His friend: No, but I've seen a man eating turkey
- my dad at Christmas!

SHEEP
What do you get if you cross a **sheep** with a
penguin and a kangaroo?
A black and white woolly jumper!

SHEEP DOGS

What do you get if you cross a **sheep dog** with a daisy?
A collieflower!

SHIP

What **ship** can't you sink?
Friendship!

SHIRT

Why did the little girl wear her **shirt** in the shower?
Because the instructions said 'wash and wear'.

SHOW JUMPING

Small girl in riding gear: When I took my pony **show jumping** we lost by a single refusal.
Impressed adult: Really?
Girl: Yes, he refused to get out of the horse box!

SHOWER

What type of cake do you take into the **shower**?
A sponge cake.

SKELETON

Why didn't the **skeleton** go to the disco?
He didn't have any body to go with!

What did the **skeleton** say to his friend in a storm?
'Oooh that wind goes straight through me.'

SKUNK

How many **skunks** do you need to make a smell?
Just a phewww!

What is smelly and extremely noisy?
A **skunk** with a drum kit.

SKYDIVING

What's the hardest thing about **skydiving**?
The ground.

SLATES

What do you call a girl with **slates** on her head?

Roof.

SLUG

Man in restaurant: Waiter, there's a **slug** in my salad.
Waiter: I'm sorry, sir, I didn't know you're a vegetarian!

SMELLY SOCKS?

IS YOUR FUNKY SMELLING FOOTWEAR FREAKING OUT YOUR FRIENDS?

FEAR NOT!

SIMPLY SEND FOR OUR **MIRACLE CURE!**

AND NOBODY WILL COMPLAIN ABOUT YOUR SOCKS EVER AGAIN!

(LET'S FACE IT, WITH OUR PONGY PANTS ON YOUR HEAD WHO'S GOING TO NOTICE YOUR SOCKS?)

SMELL

How do you stop a dead fish from **smelling**?

Hold its nose!

What is the **smelliest** city in the world?

Phew York.

SNAILS

Teacher: Where do you find giant **snails**?
Girl: *On a giant's fingers and toes!*

SNAKE

A daddy **snake** and his little son snake were wiggling down the road. 'Dad,' said the little snake suddenly. 'Are we the sort of snake that crushes people to a hideous death, or are we the sort that poisons them with our deadly venom?'
'We crush them to a hideous death, son. Why?'
'I'm so glad,' said the little snake. *'I just bit my lip!'*

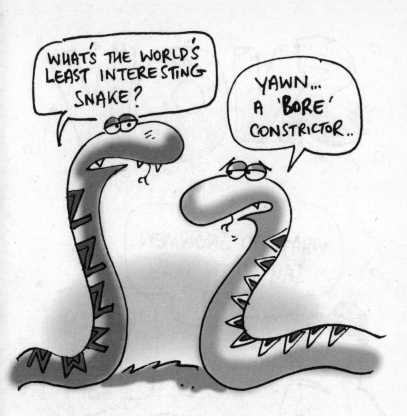

SNOOKER

Doctor, doctor, I think I'm turning into a snooker ball.
Well wait at the end of the cue then.

SNORE

A man went to the doctor: 'It's terrible doctor –
I snore so loudly that I wake myself up!'
'*Well, why don't you sleep in another room?*' asked
the doctor.

SOCKS

What's woolly and very loud?
A **socksophone**.

SOLDIERS

Which month do **soldiers** hate the most?
March.

SOLICITORS

What do **solicitors** wear in court?
Lawsuits.

SPADE

What do you call a man with a **spade** on his head?
Doug!

What do you call a man *without* a **spade** on his head?
Dougless!

SPARROW

Why did the **sparrow** get a driving ticket?
She was going down a one-way tweet.

SPECTACLES

Did hear about the optician who fell into the lens grinder?
He made a **spectacle** of himself.

SPOONS

Doctor, doctor, I think I've swallowed a **spoon**.
Well sit there and don't stir.

STAMP COLLECTORS!

PHIL ATELY HERE, THE WORLD'S TOP STAMP DEALER WITH A SUPER SPECIAL OFFER! SIMPLY SEND SEVERAL HUNDRED SMACKERS (WELL IT IS THE 'S' SECTION AFTER ALL!) AND I WILL SEND YOU <u>THE WORLD'S RAREST STAMP</u>! SIMPLE, EH? DON'T DELAY, SEND YOUR MONEY TODAY! *

* NOTE: THE REASON THIS STAMP IS SO RARE IS THAT, HAVING TAKEN YOUR MONEY, PHIL RARELY REMEMBERS TO SEND IT!

STEAK

A man was sitting in a restaurant and the waiter brought his food. The man was horrified to see that the waiter had his thumb on the **steak** that he had ordered. 'Waiter!' he snapped. 'You've got your thumb on my steak!'

'I know,' said the waiter calmly. *'But you wouldn't want it to fall on the floor again, would you?'*

STEPS

What goes ninety-nine **steps** tap, ninety-nine steps, tap?
A centipede with a wooden leg!

STEW

Lady in cafe: Waiter, is there any **stew** on the menu?
Waiter: No, madam, I wiped it off!

STICK

What do you call a boomerang that won't come back?
A stick.

STORM

What is a **storm's** favourite party game?
Twister.

STRIKE

What do you do if your nose goes on **strike**?
Picket.

STRONG

What is the world's **strongest** bird?
The crane!

SUITCASE

A man went to the doctor and told him that he thought he was turning into a **suitcase**. The doctor sent him packing.

SUN

Last night I went to bed wondering where the **sun** had gone, but this morning it dawned on me!

SURGEON

What do you call a **surgeon** with eight arms?
A doctopus.

SWEETS

Teacher: Jane, if you had ten sweets and John asked you for one, how many would you have?
Jane: Ten!

SWIMMING POOL

What do you call a man who just likes to float in the **swimming pool**?
Bob.

HEY! WHAT ARE YOU TWO DOING SITTING AND NATTERING AWAY RIGHT AT THE START OF MY SECTION?

SORRY- WE DIDN'T REALIZE THIS WAS YOUR JOKE SECTION...
YEAH- WE THOUGHT IT WAS JUST A 'T' BREAK.
G
F

TALKING DOGS

A man went into a pub and told the barman that his dog was a **talking dog**. 'I bet you five pounds I can get him to answer any question you like to ask him,' he said.

'OK,' said the barman. 'How are you?'

'Rough!' barked the dog.

'And what do you call the top of a house?'

'Roof!' barked the dog again.

'Right,' said the barman. 'Now then, who was the manager of the English football team in the last World Cup?'

'Rought!' barked the dog.

'What a load of rubbish!' said the barman. 'Give me my five pounds.'

The man gave the barman the money and started to leave the pub. On the way through the door the dog turned to the man and said,

'I remember now. It was Sven-Goran Eriksson!'

TANK

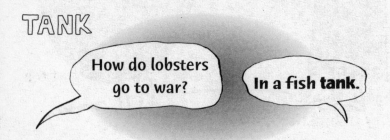

How do lobsters go to war?

In a fish **tank**.

TAR

What's black and sticky and swings through the jungle?

Tar-zan...

TARANTULA

Why do **tarantulas** have hairy legs?
Are YOU going to ask them to shave them?

TAXI

A man and his wife were getting ready to leave a restaurant and go home. 'Waiter,' he said, 'Please would you call me a **taxi**.'
'*Certainly, sir,*' said the waiter. '*You're a taxi!*'

Where would you find a stuffed **taxi**?
At the taxidermists.

TEA

DOCTOR, DOCTOR, every time I drink a mug of tea I get a pain up my nose.
'Try taking the spoon out of the mug.'

TEACHERS

Why was the **teacher** cross-eyed?
He couldn't control his pupils!

Jane: Mummy, I don't want to go to school today.
Everyone there hates me, and I don't like school
dinners, and the boys tease me and they all call
me names and things; it's horrible!
Jane's mother: Don't be silly Jane, you must go –
you're the teacher!

Teachers are special because they are in a class of
their own.

TEDDY BEARS

How do you start a **teddy bear** race?
'Ready, Teddy, GO!'

TELEPHONE

What do you get
if you **telephone**
68496837259783754968572?

A sore finger!

What did the big **telephone**, say to the little telephone?

You're too young to be engaged!

TENNIS

What do you call a girl who lies across the middle of a **tennis** court?
Annette!

Tennis is such a noisy game; the players are always raising a racket!

THEATRE

A man was sitting in the **theatre** when a large lady squeezed past him and went out to the lavatory.
As she went past she stood on his foot.
When she came back in she whispered to him:
'Excuse me, did I just stand on your foot?'
'Yes,' said the man.
'*Oh good, then this is my row,*' she replied.

THIEF

What's a good first name for a **thief**?

Rob.

THUMB

Lady in restaurant: Waiter, your thumb is in my soup!

Waiter: **Don't worry, madam, *it's not hot*!**

TICK

What goes **tick** woof, tick woof, tick woof?
A watch dog!

TICKET

Why are air **tickets** so expensive?
The fares are sky high.

TIDY

My mum is so **tidy** after she cleans the house she spends hours looking for somewhere to put the cupboards.

STOP!!
SOMETHING'S GONE TERRIBLY WRONG WITH THE BOOK! ONE OF MY 'T' ANIMALS HAS ESCAPED!
SO PLEASE DON'T TURN THE PAGE IF YOU DON'T WANT TO SEE A HORRIBLE PICTURE
OF A TIGER EATING A MAN!!

SEE? WHAT DID I TELL YOU- AND I WAS PLANNING TO HAVE THAT GINGERBREAD MAN FOR MY LUNCH, TOO. HOW HORRIBLE IS THAT?

TIGER

An explorer felt rather nervous about going into the jungle.

'Are you sure there are no **tigers** there?' he asked the native guide.

'*Certain*,' said the guide. '*The lions have chased them all away!*'

What's the quickest way to feed a **tiger**?
Just lie down in front of it.

TIME

Why did the boy throw his alarm clock out of the window?
He wanted to see if **time** flies.

'Can you give me the **time**?'
'**Three pm.**'
'It can't be – it's still morning!'
'*You didn't tell me which time you wanted.*'

My mum taught me to read the **time**.
The trouble is, those are the only two words she taught me.

TIN

What did one **tin** can say to the other tin can?
'*I've taken a bit of a shine to you.*'

TINY

What's very small but very dangerous?
A stick of **tiny**-mite.

TOMATOES

A boy came to school one morning with a huge
lump on his forehead. 'James,' said the teacher.
'However did you get that terrible bump on
the head?'
'A **tomato** fell on it, Miss.'
'A tomato!' said the teacher in amazement. 'It must
have been a mighty big tomato.'
'No, Miss,' replied James. '*It was quite small, but it
was in a tin.*'

TONGUE

A small boy rushed downstairs late one night:
'Daddy, Daddy, come quickly,' he wailed. 'There's
something under my bed, with it's **tongue**
hanging out!'
'*Don't be silly, son, that's your shoe,*' said
his father.

TONSILS

What did the **tonsils** say to each other?
'*Let's get dressed up, the doctor's going to take us
out tonight.*'

TOUCAN

What has feathers, a beak and loves reading?
A book toucan.

TOUR DE FRANCE

Did you hear about the man who won the **Tour de France**? Straight after the race he disappeared for three weeks. He was doing a lap of honour!

TOURIST ATTRACTION

London's latest **tourist attraction** is the London Contact Lens. It's just like the London Eye only you can see farther.

TOYSHOP

A lady went into a **toyshop**: 'I'd like something for my son, please,' she said.
'*Certainly, madam*,' said the assistant. '*How much were you thinking of asking?*'

TRAFFIC LIGHT

What did the **traffic light** say to the car?
'*Don't look now, I'm changing!*'

TRAINS

What do you call a **train** full of toffee?
A chew chew train.

What do you call an underground **train** full of professors?
A tube of smarties!

Will the **train** now standing on platform ten please get back on to the rails.

Don't fall asleep near a railway – **trains** run over sleepers!

TREE

What did the beaver say to the **tree**?
'*Nice to gnaw you!*'

TROLL

What are tasty, hairy and turn up in fairytales?
Sausage trolls.

TROUSERS

Teacher to scruffy boy: Jimmy, you've got holes in your **trousers**.
Jimmy: **Of course I have, otherwise how could I get my legs into them?**

TURKEYS

How do farmyard animals communicate with each other?
By walkie-turkey.

TEST YOUR J.Q...
What do you get if you cross a Turtle with a Vampire?
a Terror-pin!

TURTLES

What do **turtles** walk about on in the evening?
Bedroom flippers.

TV

'My mum lets me watch the **TV** all day.'
'**Wow, that's really nice of her!**'
'No, not really. She won't let me turn it on.'

TWIT

How do you keep a **twit** in suspense?
I don't know, please tell me… go on… tell me.

UDDER

What has four legs, an **udder** and flies?
A cow!

UFO

How do smelly aliens travel?
In a Phew·F·O.

ULTRAVIOLET

What is a crook's favourite colour?
Ultraviolent.

UMBRELLA

What do bees use to keep the rain off?
Humbrellas.

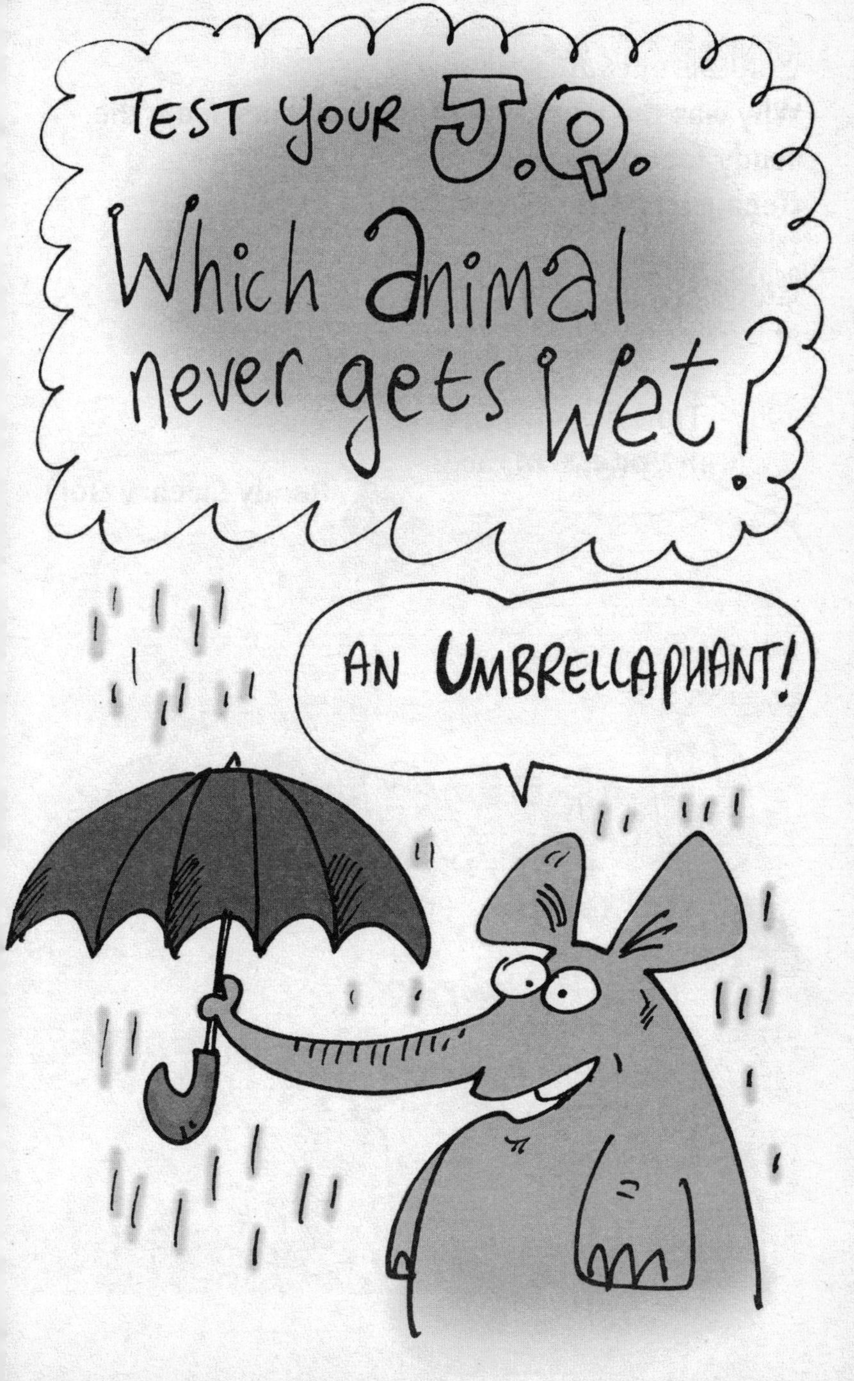
TEST YOUR J.Q.
Which animal never gets wet?
AN UMBRELLAPHANT!

UNBEARABLE

Why was the truckload of fur sent back from the Teddy factory?

Because it was **unbearable**.

UNDERARM

How do you start an **underarm** race?

Ready Sweaty Go!

UNDERTAKER

Who do you call in when your Y-fronts have died?
The **undie-taker**.

UNHAPPY

What do you do to an **unhappy** table?
Chair it up.

UNIVERSE

What kind of poetry do aliens write?
Universe.
He wanted to shine in his exams.

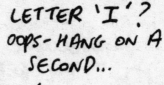

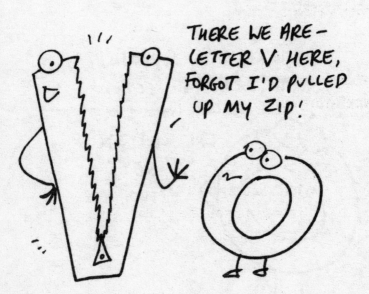

VACATION

Where do fireflies go on **vacation**?
The Ignited Kingdom.

VACCINATION

What's the world's healthiest nation?
The **vaccin-nation**.

VACUUM

Why do **vacuum** cleaners never have any money?
They are always being taken for suckers.

VALENTINE

How do you fix a broken heart?
With **valen-twine**.

VAMPIRES

What's a **vampire's** favourite food?
Neck-tarines!

What's a **vampire's** favourite soup?

Scream of mushroom!

VANDALIZE

How do you **vandalize** a pair of shoes?
With gra-feet-i.

VANISH

Shopper: Have you got any **vanishing** cream?
Shop assistant: Yes, of course...hang on it was
there a minute ago.

VAPOUR

How do ghosts wipe their bottoms?
With toilet **vapour**.

VARNISH

Why did the pupil paint himself with **varnish**?
He wanted to shine in his exams.

VATICAN

What's the most popular snack in the **Vatican**?
Pope-corn.

VAULT

How did the banker get locked in the money store?
Through no **vault** of his own.

VEGETABLE

Did you hear about the **vegetable** truck
that crashed?
Ye – it was a carrot-tastrophe.

280

VEST

What did the policeman say to his belly button?
You're under a vest!

VICAR

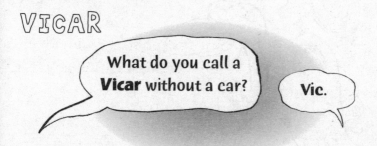

What do you call a **Vicar** without a car?

Vic.

VIOLIN

Did you hear about the girl who was so unmusical that it took her a year to get a sound out of a **violin**? For the first eleven months she blew it...

VIPER

Why didn't the **viper** viper nose?
'Cos the adder 'ad 'er 'andkerchief.

VOCAL CHORDS

What kind of trousers do singers wear?
Vocal chords.

VOLCANO

What did one **volcano** say to the other?
Do you lava me like I lava you?

... BECAUSE IT'S VERY HARD TO KEEP THE INTERNET WORKING NOW THAT THE THREE Ws HAVE GONE MISSING!

OUT OF ORDER

DRONE! DRONE! DRONE! DRONE! DRONE! DRONE! DRONE! DRONE! DRONE! DRONE! DRONE! DRONE! DRONE! DRONE! DRONE! DRONE! DRONE! DRONE! DRONE! DRONE!
NOTE TO AUTHOR FROM PUBLISHER:
Thank you for inviting your teacher to lecture on this page but actually the 'waffle' joke we asked for was supposed to be about the kind you eat!

WALLY

Wally couldn't tell his two cows apart but one day he wondered if one of them might be just slightly taller than the other one. He measured them and sure enough, the black and white one was an inch taller than the brown one!

WATCH

A girl was showing her new **watch** to a friend in the playground.
'Look at this watch – it's amazing. My dad gave it to me, it cost ninety pence at the garage.'
'What's amazing about it?' asked the friend.
'It's amazing that it's still going!'

My **watch** won't tell me the time. I just can't get it to speak.

My **watch** has got a 'cheese' alarm.
It keeps going off.

WATER

Have you heard about the man who gave up **water** skiing?
He couldn't find any sloping lakes.

When is **water** not water?
When it's dripping!

Teacher: Spell **water**.
Boy: HIJKLMNO.
Teacher: That doesn't spell water.
Boy: Yes, it does - it's all the letters from H to O!

WATER RATS
Where do **water rats** keep their money?
In river banks!

WEASELS
Fascinating fact It's easy to tell
the difference between **weasels** and stoats.
Weasels are weaselly wecognized and stoats are
stoatally different.

WEDDING
A small boy was at his big sister's **wedding**. When
the vicar asked who was giving the bride away, he
piped up, *'Why, what's she done wrong?'*

WEIGHT TRAINING
Girl: My stupid brother does **weight training**.
Her friend: Really?
Girl: Yes, he stands about and waits for trains!

WELL
A man fell down a deep **well**. 'Have you broken
anything?' his friend called down to him.
'No, there's nothing down here to break!' replied
the man.

WARNING!
If you are of a n-nervous n-nature you may w-want to skip the n-next p-page...
GET READY FOR A GENUINE PICTURE OF THE SCARIEST W OF ALL....
A WILD, WILD
WEREWOLF!

SORRY FOLKS, THIS IS A PICTURE OF A WILD WEREWOLF... UNFORTUNATELY HE'S SO WILD HE LIVES IN THE ARCTIC SNOW AND HAS TOTALLY WHITE FUR...

WETTER

What gets **wetter** the more it dries?

A towel.

WHISPER

Why is **whispering** banned?
Because it's not aloud.

WILD CATS

Which **wild cats** look good in suits?
Cuff lynx.

WILMA

Knock! Knock!
'Who's there?'
'**Wilma**.'
'Wilma who?'
'Will ma mum come out and let me in?'

WIND

DOCTOR, DOCTOR, I've got **wind**, can you give me something for it?
Yes, how about a kite...

WINDOW

A man wasn't feeling very well so he went to the doctor. 'OK,' said the doctor when he had examined him. 'I want you to turn and face the **window**, and stick your tongue out.'
'Will that cure me?' said the man.
'No,' said the doctor. 'But I don't like the man who lives in the house opposite!'

WINDOW SHOPPING

Did you hear about the man who went
window shopping?
He came back with five windows.

WINE GLASSES

'Mummy, I'm going to buy you a lovely set of **wine glasses** for Christmas,' said little Jason.
'That's very kind, dear, but I've already got a set of wine glasses.'
'You haven't,' said Jason sadly. 'I've just dropped them.'

WITCHES

Why are **witches** good at English?

They are brilliant at spelling!

An old **witch** thought that she would make a fortune telling fortunes, so she bought a crystal ball, but she couldn't see any future in it!

What **witches** do you find in the desert?

Sandwitches!

I met two **witches** who were twins - I just couldn't tell witch witch was which!

WOBBLE

What lies in a pram and wobbles?
A jellybaby!

What flies and wobbles?
A jellicopter!

WOOD

A boy was working in a carpentry lesson.
'Please, sir,' he said to the woodwork teacher,
'I need some more **wood**.'
'MORE wood!' said the teacher in amazement.
'Wood doesn't grow on trees you know!'

WOODWORK

Did you hear about the **woodwork** teacher who broke all his teeth?
He bit his nails!

WOODWORM

Fascinating fact: 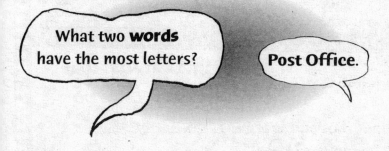 If you cross a **woodworm** with an elephant, you get very big holes in your furniture.

WORDS

What two **words** have the most letters?

Post Office.

A boy showed his school report to his father and then took it to his mother. 'What did your dad say when he'd read it?' she asked.
'**Can I use rude words?**'
'No, of course not.'
'**He didn't say anything then,**' said the boy.

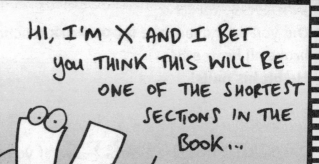

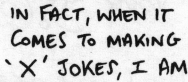

TEST YOUR J.Q.

What Test do you only PASS by getting all the WRONG ANSWERS?

AN "X-AM"!

X

There aren't many jokes beginning with X.
Yes, but I don't know Y...

X-RATED JOKES

What's green and hangs from trees?
Giraffe snot!

Why was the beach wet?
Because the seaweed.

What's yellow and smells of bananas?
Monkey sick!

Where do you find a dog with no legs?
The last place you put it!

Someone in class made a rude noise. 'Stop that!'
said the teacher.
'OK,' said one of his pupils. 'Which way did it go?'

What's the difference between a letterbox and a
cow's bottom?
I don't know.
Well I wouldn't ask you to post a letter for me then!

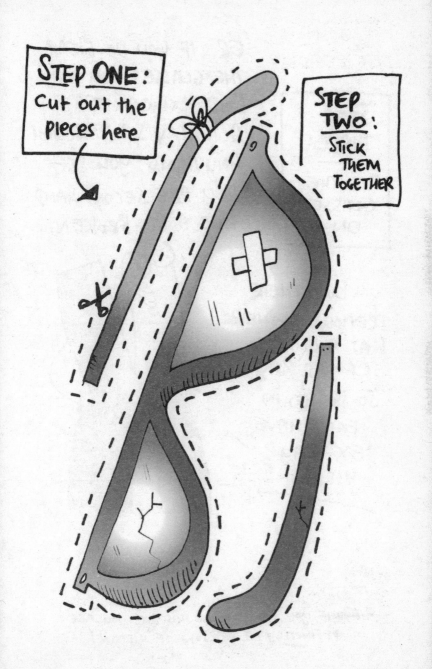

STEP THREE:

PUT THE GLASSES ON!

ER... IF YOU DO WEAR THE GLASSES YOU MAY FIND YOU CAN'T ACTUALLY SEE THROUGH ANYTHING. YOU SEE THEY ARE SECOND HAND AND A BIT BROKEN...

... BUT THEIR PREVIOUS OWNER WAS A GUY CALLED 'RAY', SO YOU DO IN FACT HAVE 'EX-RAY' VISION! *

* AND IF YOU SAW THROUGH THIS JOKE YOU ARE DEFINITELY A PERSON OF VISION!

XYLOPHONE

What's a dentist's favourite music instrument?
A smile-ophone.

What's a mummy's favourite musical instrument?
A Nile-ophone.

What's a really bad musician's favourite
instrument?
A Vile-ophone.

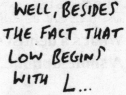

YAK

What's the world's most talkative animal?
The yak.

YAWN

How do you cut down on yawning?
With a **yawn**-mower.

YELLOW

What's **yellow** and dangerous?
Shark infested
custard!

What's **yellow** on the inside and green
on the outside?
A banana dressed up as a cucumber!

What's **yellow** and white and goes down railway
tracks at a hundred miles an hour?
A train driver's egg sandwich.

What's **yellow** and writes?
A ball-point banana.

YELP

How do dogs learn to bark?
With a little yelp from their friends.

YEW

What did one evergreen tree say to the other
evergreen tree?
What are yew looking at?

YONDER

What do long distance walkers wear under their trousers?
Yonder-pants.

YO-YO

Newsflash: A ship loaded with **yo-yoes** has hit a rock. It sank fifty-two times.

YOUNG LADY

*There was a **young lady** from Riga*
Who rode, with a smile, on a tiger!
They returned from the ride
With the lady inside,
And the smile on the face of the tiger!

YULE

Where does Santa go for a swim?

In the **yule**-tide.

OH YEAH?
SUCH AS...

SUCH AS... WHY
DID THE 'Z' CROSS
THE ROAD?

IS THAT THE
FIRST JOKE?

NO - I
LEFT
MY LIST
OF JOKES
ON THE
OTHER SIDE
OF THE
ROAD. HANG
ON FOLKS —
BACK IN A
MINUTE!

ZAMBIA

What's the world's scariest country?
Zombia.

ZAP

What do you say to a laser on its birthday?
Many **Zappy** Returns.

ZEBRA

Why weren't there any **zebras** in the zoo?
They had all gone on stripe.

What's black and white and sneaky?
A **zebra** double crossing.

What do you call a **zebra** with no stripes?
A horse!

What did the silly man call his **zebra**?

Spot!

What's black and white and goes round and r
A **zebra** in a revolving door!

What's black and white and red all over?
An embarrassed zebra!

What do you get if you cross a **zebra** with a sheep?
A stripy sweater.

What do you get if you cross a **zebra** with a sheep
and a kangaroo?
A stripy sweater with pockets.

ZERO
Why was the **zero** punished?
Because it was noughty.

ZIGZAG
What's a gazgiz?
A zigzag line drawn backwards.

ZINC
What happened when there was a flood in the
chemistry lab?
It was zinc or swim.

ZIP
What did one **zip** fastener say to the other
zip fastener?
Pull yourself together.

ZOO
Newsflash: Precious birds have been stolen from the **zoo**. The Flying Squad are looking into it.

ZOMBIE
What's scary and stings?
A **zom-bee**.

ZZUB ZZUB
What goes **zzub zzub**?
A bee flying backwards!

TEST YOUR JQ...
Was the Z exhausted after all the jokes in this Book?

YOU 'ZED' IT....

ZZZZZZ